CONTEN.

D0191276

About this book vi
About the author ix
Acknowledgements xi

Introduction 1

1 What is cloud computing? 3

Three layers of computing 4
Defining cloud computing 6
Essential characteristics 7
Three service models 10
Four deployment models 16
When is a cloud not a cloud? 17
Twelve adoption scenarios 18
Quick technology tips 18
Summary 22
Key summary points 23
Question and activity 24

2 Benefits of cloud computing 25

Financial benefits 26
Technological benefits 28
Operational features and benefits 30
Environmental benefits 33
Competitive advantage 35
Summary 37
Key summary points 37
Question and activity 38

3 Risks of cloud computing 39

Internal security risks 40

External security risks 43

Data protection risks 45

Cloud outages 47

Data loss 49

Vendor lock-in 50

Vendor failure 52

Risk calculator 52

Summary 54

Key summary points 54

Question and activity 55

4 Case studies 57

SaaS case studies 58

PaaS case studies 64

IaaS case studies 66

Size matters in the cloud 67

Summary 74

Key summary points, question and activity 75

5 Choosing a provider 77

The crowded cloud marketplace 78

Client references 82

Service level agreements 83

Service costs 90

Processes, practices and standards 97

Summary and checklist 97

Key summary points and checklist 98

Question and activity 99

6 Moving into the cloud 101

Step 1: Investigation 102

Step 2: Evaluation 107

Step 3: Decision 109
Step 4: Implementation 110
Step 5: Iteration 114
Summary 115
Key summary points 115
Question and activity 116

7 Conclusion 117
Obstacles to adoption 118
Predictions 119
Top ten tips 121

Glossary 123
References 135

ABOUT THIS BOOK

This *Quick Start Guide* aims to cut through the industry hype and confusion surrounding cloud computing, create understanding and help executives to select those cloud computing solutions and service providers, if any, that can best improve the way they do business. Technical terms are used where necessary, but the terminology is introduced gradually and a glossary is provided at the rear of the book. If you are involved in directing IT strategy then this book contains tips, tools and checklists that can help you make the right choices for your business and reject 'solutions' that fix problems you do not have.

BUSINESS ISSUES

Common business issues covered in this book include:

- IT system complexity and the associated administration overheads.
- Capital cost reduction and cash flow management.
- Business continuity and disaster recovery.
- Responding quickly to changes in economic conditions.
- Providing a modern, reliable service to customers.
- Data security and data protection on the internet.
- Rapid provisioning of IT systems.

- Better time management through more efficient systems and processes.
- Risk management.
- Information governance.
- Vendor lock-in fears.
- Supporting a remote and mobile workforce.
- Energy efficiency and climate change.

STRUCTURE

The book is structured as follows:

- Chapter 1 explains what cloud computing is, introduces the three main service models, and presents example adoption scenarios.
- Chapter 2 explores the potential benefits of cloud computing to your business and the environment.
- Chapter 3 details some of the risks associated with cloud computing and suggests ways to mitigate these risks.
- Chapter 4 contains a number of case studies from businesses big and small.
- Chapter 5 provides guidance on how to find and choose a service provider.
- Chapter 6 suggests a five-step process for moving your business into the cloud.
- Chapter 7 concludes the book with a summary, some predictions and ten top tips for cloud adoption.

Each chapter closes with a list of key summary points, a question for you to answer and a suggested activity for you to complete. These features are intended to help you relate what you have read to your particular business requirements.

Please note that I have avoided listing numerous examples of service providers that were prominent at the time of writing, because the cloud computing landscape changes so rapidly. However, Chapter 5 lists directories of cloud computing providers and these are a good starting point.

ABOUT THE AUTHOR

I began my postgraduate career in 1992 as a particle physicist based at CERN, birthplace of the Worldwide Web, before switching to a similar facility (SLAC) in California in 1998. At SLAC I managed a major intranet redevelopment project, which inspired me to form my first company, Surfability, in 2000 with the help of an Enterprise Fellowship award from The Royal Society of Edinburgh. A partnership with an early cloud computing provider, Extrasys, led to employment in 2005 with their new owners, and I went on to run the Extrasys business before helping to sell it on again in 2009. I now operate a consulting practice, Muon Consulting, and I blog about cloud computing at http://blog.muoncloud.com.

During the past two decades I have witnessed the birth of web technologies and vast computing grids in scientific laboratories, and I have been amazed at how these tools have become so wonderfully rich and mature – powered by computer science but driven by business – and made their way into the office and the home. I now look forward to the next 20 years as cloud computing takes us into a new era where every business has access to increasingly powerful computing resources on a pay-per-use basis.

PRACTISING WHAT I PREACH

I used cloud computing to write this book. Original diagrams were drawn using Gliffy (http://www.gliffy.com) and the manuscript was backed up automatically to Amazon's Simple Storage Service using Dropbox (http://www.dropbox.com).

ACKNOWLEDGEMENTS

The author would like to thank Fiona, Isla and Caitlin for their support and patience while this book was being put together; Lucy Handley and Niall Sclater for their willingness to be interviewed; Jaydeep Korde for introducing him to the cloud computing business; and Mike Spink for his expert review of an early manuscript.

INTRODUCTION

The rise of the cloud is more than just another platform shift that gets geeks excited. It will undoubtedly transform the IT industry, but it will also profoundly change the way people work and companies operate.

The Economist, 'Let it Rise', October 2008

According to a press release from Gartner, Inc. announcing their *2009 Hype Cycle Special Report*, 'The levels of hype around cloud computing in the IT industry are deafening, with every vendor expounding its cloud strategy, and variations, such as private cloud computing and hybrid approaches, compounding the hype' (Pettey and Stevens, 2009a). They also forecast in 2009 that the global market for cloud services would grow to $150.1 billion per year by 2013, almost a three-fold increase on their estimated market size for 2009 (Pettey and Stevens, 2009b). Now, Gartner is an internationally renowned IT research and advisory company, but is the hype they have rightfully observed actually deserved, and what is cloud computing anyway?

ABOUT CLOUD COMPUTING

'Cloud computing' has caused a marketing fog as competing IT solution vendors redefine this seemingly simple term in their own image – a practice called 'cloud washing' – making it difficult for business executives to appreciate the fundamental *paradigm shift* that true cloud computing services bring to IT. Chapter 1 will provide a detailed explanation and a definition of cloud computing, but here is Gartner's concise and much quoted definition, which is packed with concepts: 'Cloud computing is a style of computing where scalable and elastic IT-enabled capabilities are provided "as a service" to multiple external customers using Internet technologies.' In simple terms, cloud computing enables businesses of all sizes to quickly procure and use a wide range of enterprise-class IT systems on a pay-per-use basis from anywhere at any time.

CHAPTER 1
WHAT IS CLOUD COMPUTING?

The interesting thing about cloud computing is that we've redefined cloud computing to include everything that we already do. I can't think of anything that isn't cloud computing with all of these announcements. The computer industry is the only industry that is more fashion-driven than women's fashion. Maybe I'm an idiot, but I have no idea what anyone is talking about. What is it? It's complete gibberish. It's insane. When is this idiocy going to stop?

Larry Ellison, CEO, Oracle, September 2008

Even in the IT industry there is no consensus on what 'cloud computing' actually means, and some industry heavyweights and critics consider the term meaningless and have been vehemently opposed to its use. Despite these objections the term has become widely adopted and even Larry Ellison went on to say: 'We'll make cloud computing announcements. I'm not going to fight this thing. But I don't understand what we would do differently in the light of cloud' (Farber, 2008).

But in many ways the meaninglessness of the term 'cloud computing' is itself *meaningful*. We can wrap up the technical concepts of this kind of computing into a nice fluffy 'cloud', which somehow makes it less scary and more appealing. The internet itself has traditionally been depicted as a cloud in network diagrams, and, just like the internet, business users do not need to know how it works, they just need to understand what they can do with it.

In this chapter I will present a simple three-layer model of computing in general before defining and describing cloud computing in light of this model. I will then work through a list of common adoption scenarios and compare cloud-based IT solutions with non-cloud solutions to illustrate the differences. As we shall see, there is more to cloud computing than clever technology; to IT buyers it represents a radically different way of procuring a full range of IT capabilities on a *pay-per-use* basis.

THREE LAYERS OF COMPUTING

At a basic level when you use a personal computer you interact with three layers of computing. First, at the lowest layer, you have a physical piece of hardware with its processors, memory chips, disk drives, network cards and other components – we can call this the *infrastructure*. Second, in the middle layer, you have an operating system (such as Microsoft Windows) that interacts with the hardware and provides a consistent environment for running and developing software (using Visual Basic or Microsoft Access, for example) if you wish – we can call this the *platform*. And finally, at the top, there are third-party software applications (such as word processing packages) that you use in your work and play – and we can call these *software*. Figure 1.1

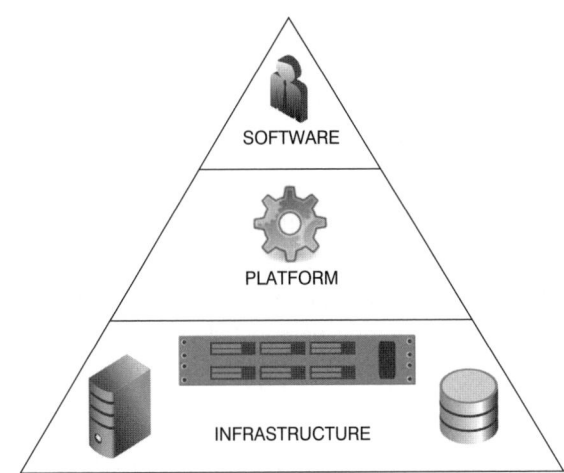

FIGURE 1.1 A simple three-layer pyramid model of computing

depicts this three-layer model of computing as a *pyramid* with infrastructure at the bottom, the platform in the middle and software at the top.

Now consider a computer network for an office-based business that manages its own IT systems. To run this network the business would typically require system administrators to look after hardware and networking (infrastructure); IT support staff and desktop deployment tools to install applications and update the operating systems (platforms) on desktop computers; and users who perform tasks with these applications (software).

This three-layer model can be applied to *cloud computing*, too, but there are a few key differences:

- *Software* applications are not desktop applications – they are web-based so they can be used in any up-to-date web browser on any computer operating system.

- *Platforms* are purpose-built software development environments that are hosted on the internet rather than your desktop computer so all you need is a web browser to create, test and deploy web applications.

- *Infrastructure* elements (servers, storage, bandwidth, processing power, etc) are provided by a third party; but you can access and use these computing resources as if they were installed on your own corporate network.

Like Michael Sheehan, who first proposed a 'cloud pyramid', I find the three-layer model useful for differentiating between cloud computing service offerings (Sheehan, 2008).

DEFINING CLOUD COMPUTING

I have already opined in the introduction that cloud computing has led to a 'marketing fog', and this is no better illustrated than with the multitude of definitions for the term. I considered a number of well-known definitions of cloud computing, but I have chosen the NIST (National Institute of Standards and Technology) draft definition as my preferred definition because it is publicly available, it reflects the IT market and it is relatively simple, in my opinion. Quoting from draft number 15 (Mell and Grance, 2009):

Cloud computing is a model for enabling convenient, on-demand network access to a shared pool of configurable computing resources (eg networks, servers, storage, applications, and services) that can be rapidly provisioned and released with minimal management effort or service provider interaction.

This cloud model promotes availability and is composed of five essential characteristics, three service models, and four deployment models.

The NIST draft definition goes on to describe these five essential characteristics (on-demand self-service, broad network access, resource pooling, rapid elasticity and measured service), three service models (Software as a Service – SaaS, Platform as a Service – PaaS and Infrastructure as a Service – IaaS), and four deployment models (Private, Community, Public and Hybrid Cloud); but this chapter provides alternative descriptions. See Figure 1.2 for a visual representation of the NIST definition and visit http://csrc.nist.gov/groups/SNS/cloud-computing for the latest draft.

Now, some industry experts do not like the use of the SaaS, PaaS and IaaS acronyms, but they are so firmly embedded in the cloud computing literature that they cannot be ignored so I will continue to refer to them in this book. For an alternative viewpoint I refer you to 'Above the Clouds', the 2009 technical report from the University of Berkeley (Armbrust *et al*, 2009).

ESSENTIAL CHARACTERISTICS

The NIST draft definition lists five essential characteristics of cloud computing and goes on to explain what they are in technical terms (Mell and Grance, 2009). I have provided my own slightly simplified interpretations below, and when I refer to computing resources I mean such things as storage, processing, memory, network bandwidth, software applications and virtual machines.

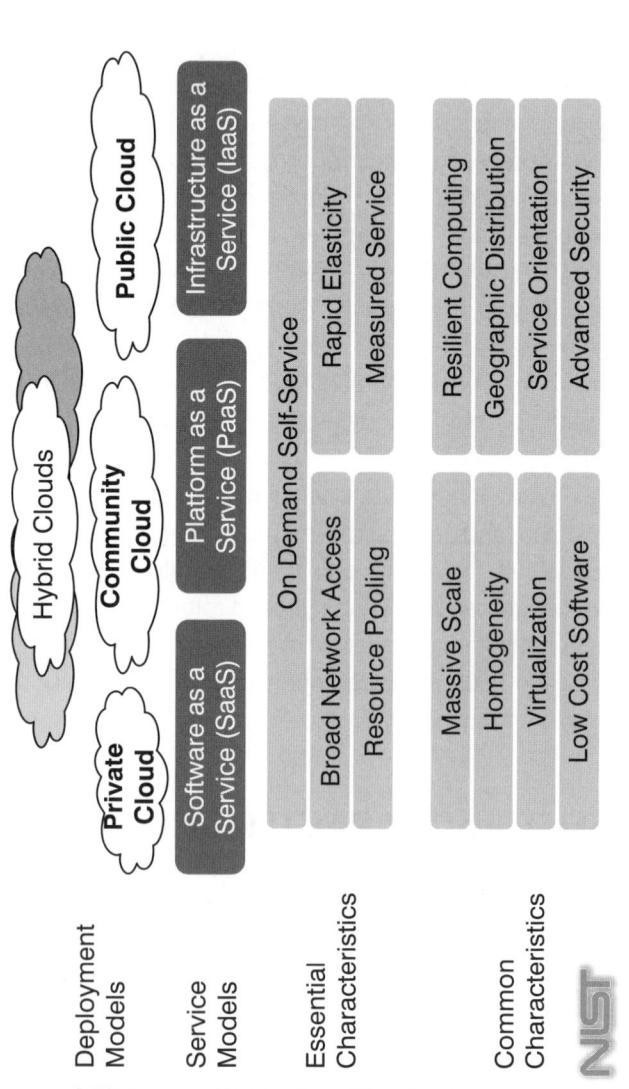

FIGURE 1.2 The NIST cloud computing definition framework

On-demand self-service

Consumers can log on to a website or use web services to access additional computing resources *on demand*, that is, whenever they want them, without talking to a sales representative or technical support staff.

Broad network access

Because they are *web-based*, you can access cloud computing services from any internet-connected device. With a web browser on a PC (or even a thin client computer terminal) you can do anything, but there is also, in many cases, explicit support for popular hand-held devices such as Blackberries and iPhones.

Resource pooling

In multi-tenanted computing clouds the customers (tenants) *share a pool of computing resources* with other customers, and these resources, which can be dynamically reallocated, may be hosted anywhere.

Rapid elasticity

Cloud computing enables computing resources or user accounts to be rapidly and *elastically* provisioned or released so that customers can scale their systems (and costs) up and down at any time according to their changing requirements.

Measured service

Cloud computing providers automatically monitor and record the resources used by customers or currently assigned to customers, which makes possible the pay-per-use billing model that is fundamental to the cloud computing paradigm.

THREE SERVICE MODELS

Different types of cloud computing are provided 'as a service' to consumers, and most of them fall under one or more of three categories: Software as a Service, Platform as a Service, and Infrastructure as a Service. It is the *service* nature of cloud computing that makes it such a disruptive force in the IT industry. Computing capabilities are rented and no hardware or software assets are purchased outright by the consumer.

Software as a Service (SaaS)

Software as a Service provides complete business applications delivered over the web. Advances in web technology such as Ajax, along with ubiquitous internet access, have made it possible to deliver the rich features and functionality of desktop applications in a web browser. SaaS applications also make use of standards for web services, and these standards enable them to easily 'call on the services' of other applications somewhere else on the web in order to exchange, include or 'mash up' data. The time savings that come with on-demand software, where nothing needs to be installed on a PC and new users can be added easily – along with the pay-per-use business model – have made SaaS a success.

The most popular and familiar example of SaaS is e-mail in a web browser, but SaaS applications are becoming increasingly sophisticated and collaborative. You can run the entire administrative, operational and sales side of your business in the cloud. SaaS capabilities provided online include tools for:

- accessing virtual Microsoft Windows desktops on a per-user-per-month rental basis;
- accounting, financial management, inventory and e-commerce;
- collaborations between employees and clients on projects;
- creating flowcharts, diagrams, floor plans and other technical drawings;
- Customer Relationships Management (CRM);
- editing, storing and sharing documents, presentations, spreadsheets, blogs, web pages and videos;
- project management;
- web-mail, calendaring, instant messaging, video conferencing and social networking.

There are many specialized SaaS applications available to rent online but some SaaS vendors provide extensive software suites (see Figure 1.3 for an example) and 'marketplaces' for integrated third-party applications (see Figure 1.4 for an example).

Platform as a Service (PaaS)

Platform as a Service provides consumers with a stable online environment where they can quickly create, test and deploy web applications using browser-based software development tools. There is less work involved in creating an application using PaaS than the traditional approach,

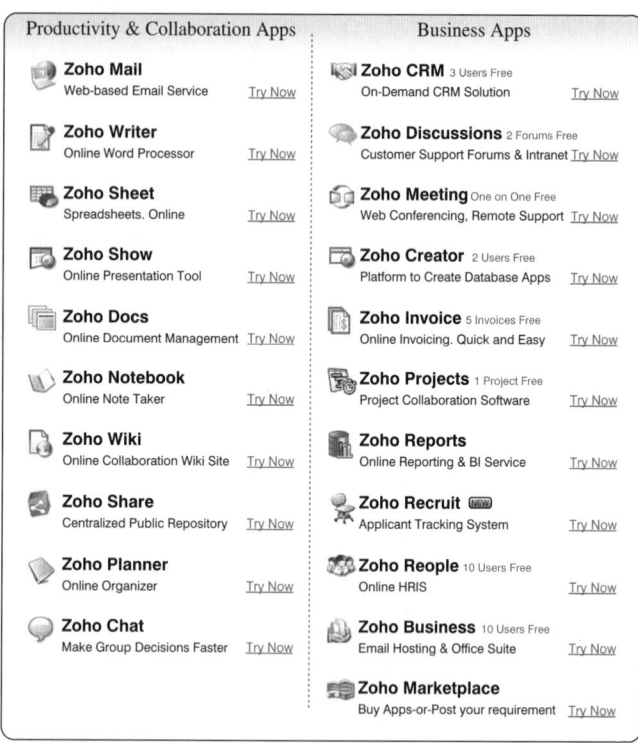

FIGURE 1.3 SaaS applications available from Zoho.com (January 2010)

which involves procuring and managing one or more servers for development, testing and production, and installing and configuring server software.

PaaS systems typically include some or all of the following features:

- browser-based development environment for creating databases and editing application code – either directly or through visual, point-and-click tools;

- built-in scalability, security, access control and web service interfaces;

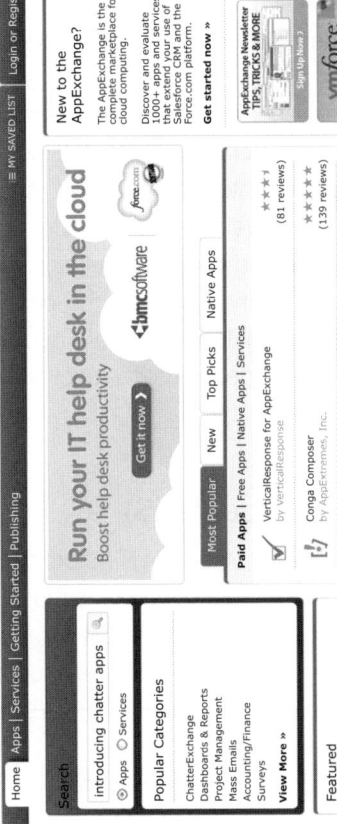

FIGURE 1.4 A screenshot of The AppExchange On-Demand Marketplace (May 2010)

- easy integration with other applications on the same platform;
- tools for connecting to applications outside the platform's cloud;
- tools for designing web forms, defining business rules and creating workflows.

If your business has its own software development team, and you are considering the cloud for application development and hosting, then your team's programming language preferences may sway your choice of PaaS provider, but software developers are accustomed to change so let this not be your only decision criterion. Moreover, some PaaS solutions enable non-developers to create web applications using visual, point-and-click tools rather than a programming language, and some give you the *best of both worlds* so you can use visual tools to create applications and a programming language to extend functionality if required.

Infrastructure as a Service (IaaS)

Software as a Service was quite a hot topic in IT before cloud computing engulfed the industry, but it was Infrastructure as a Service (IaaS) that caused the fire to take hold. IaaS provides consumers with administrative, web-based access to *fundamental* computing resources such as processing power, storage and networks.

All cloud infrastructures depend on *virtualization*. By abstracting server software from the underlying hardware, multiple virtual machines, including operating systems, storage and installed software, can run on a single physical computer and share its processing power. In cloud computing, server virtualization is extended further, going beyond the more efficient use of a single physical machine or cluster to the aggregation and partitioning of computing resources across multiple data centres. This enables cloud providers to efficiently manage and offer on-demand storage, servers and software resources for many different customers simultaneously. More importantly the web interfaces they provide empower their customers to administer computing resources as if they owned them.

IaaS systems typically include some or all of the following features:

- a choice of ready-made virtual machines with pre-installed operating systems including numerous versions of Windows, Linux and Solaris;

- a choice of virtual appliances – virtual machines with specific sets of software pre-installed;

- ability to store copies of particular data in different locations around the world to make downloads of the data as fast as possible;

- software tools to help process large amounts of data (in Data Grids) and perform complex calculations (in Compute Grids) using large arrays of virtual servers working in parallel on the same problem;

- ability to manually increase or decrease the computing resources assigned to you using a web browser as your requirements change;

- ability to automatically scale computing resources up and down in response to increases and decreases in application usage.

The elastic capability of IaaS systems makes on-demand computing possible, but it is the low entry costs and the pay-per-use charging model that make it attractive to businesses.

FOUR DEPLOYMENT MODELS

Many industry experts dispute the validity of the four deployment models in the NIST definition framework, which are
discussed below; that is, public clouds, community clouds,
private clouds and hybrid clouds. For them only public
clouds are true clouds, but when the user experience
and functional capabilities are the same, and there is the
possibility of moving seamlessly across cloud boundaries,
the distinctions become, well, *cloudy*.

Public clouds

Public cloud computing services are provided off-premise
by third-party providers to the general public and the
computing resources are shared with the provider's other
customers. This is pure cloud computing and there is no
debate on this one.

Community clouds

Community clouds are used by distinct groups (or 'communities') of organizations that have shared concerns such
as compliance or security considerations, and the computing infrastructures may be provided by internal or third-party
suppliers. The communities benefit from public cloud capabilities but they also know who their neighbours are so they
have fewer fears about security and data protection.

Private clouds

Many large organizations prefer, or are legally obligated,
to keep their servers, software and data within their own
data centres; and private clouds enable them to achieve

some of the efficiencies of cloud computing while taking responsibility for the security of their own data. By implementing cloud computing technologies behind their firewall, enterprises can enable pooling and sharing of computing resources across different applications, departments or business units. Unlike the pay-as-you-go model of public clouds, however, private clouds require significant up-front development costs, data centre costs, ongoing maintenance, hardware, software and internal expertise.

Hybrid clouds

Many enterprises take the 'hybrid cloud' approach by using public clouds for general computing while customer data is kept within a private cloud, community cloud or a more traditional IT infrastructure. The use of 'virtual private cloud' technology enables enterprises to connect their existing infrastructure to a set of isolated computing resources in a public cloud infrastructure and to extend their existing *internal* IT management capabilities – such as security services, firewalls, and intrusion detection systems – to include their *external* virtual resources. This option is attractive to businesses that have invested in their own IT infrastructure or have data protection responsibilities, but would like to take advantage of the scalability and flexibility that cloud computing affords.

WHEN IS A CLOUD NOT A CLOUD?

If there is some debate about the four deployment models then there is general agreement among IT professionals, if not marketing executives, that the following situations do not constitute cloud computing:

- renting dedicated server hardware in a data centre for a single task, such as hosting a website, even if it is on a subscription basis;

- server virtualization (running multiple virtual computers on a single server) in itself, unless servers can be deployed and destroyed in minutes by the consumer themselves rather than the provider;

- connecting to your home PC or office PC from anywhere using remote desktop or VPN (Virtual Private Network) technology.

TWELVE ADOPTION SCENARIOS

Businesses vary greatly in size, sector and maturity, and they can have very different IT requirements. Chapter 4 provides a selection of real-life case studies for Software, Platform and Infrastructure as a Service (SaaS, PaaS and IaaS); but Table 1.1 below lists common adoption scenarios where a choice could be made between cloud computing solutions and non-cloud solutions. The scenarios are wide-ranging, but they all serve to demonstrate the relative convenience of IT solutions in *public clouds* where capital investment in hardware and software by the customer is not necessary.

QUICK TECHNOLOGY TIPS

The particular cloud computing technologies you choose (if any) depend on your working practices, your business size, your current IT systems and the skills of your internal staff. All these points will be covered in later chapters, but

TABLE 1.1 Non-cloud and public cloud solutions for 12 common IT requirements

Requirement	Non-cloud solution	Public cloud solution
Start-up business needs e-mail, file sharing and office applications for varying numbers of employees and contractors	Set up an e-mail server and a VPN for file sharing; install necessary software on employee computers and ask contractors to provide their own office application software	Use an online office application software suite (SaaS)
Office PCs or laptop computers are a few years old and running desktop software slowly, but the software is old, too, and needs replacing	Upgrade computers and install new, improved desktop software	Choose SaaS and run it in a web browser on existing computer hardware
Remote working capability to enable employees to use the same desktop software and data as they have in the office	Set up VPN connections to allow remote desktop connections and network drive access or use a third-party service to connect to PCs in the office from anywhere	Use virtual hosted desktops accessible from anywhere (including office and home) or switch to other SaaS solutions

TABLE 1.1 Continued

Requirement	Non-cloud solution	Public cloud solution
Mobile working capability	Modify key IT systems to make them accessible from mobile devices such as 'smart' phones	Use SaaS to get ready-made mobile working solutions
New Customer Relationship Management (CRM) system for sales staff	Set up one or more servers for the CRM database and install desktop software on users' computers (if required)	Use a SaaS CRM which can be accessed via a web browser
Security fears surrounding data stored on laptop computers taken out of the office	Encrypt key data stored on laptops so that they cannot be accessed without a password	Store and access data in the cloud using SaaS without downloading it onto laptops
Need to collaborate effectively with partner companies online	Install third-party or in-house developed software on a web server	Choose and use SaaS collaboration software or develop new software with PaaS

TABLE 1.1 Continued

Requirement	Non-cloud solution	Public cloud solution
Software development required to manage enterprise business processes	Set up numerous servers for development, testing and production	Use a cloud-based software development platform (PaaS) that supports systems integration
Distribute new business software application to customers	Create a desktop software application and sell it online or in DVD form	Create web-based software using PaaS that can be sold on the platform provider's online market place
New marketing campaign will temporarily overload current web server	Upgrade server and bandwidth to cope with a large number of hits in a short space of time	Move website to an elastic public cloud (IaaS) so it can respond dynamically to highs and lows in web traffic
Automated backups for IT systems and business data	Set up a secondary data centre to copy backups to	Use IaaS to back up data and virtual servers
Run a large and complex computer simulation	Use all available computing hardware for as long as it takes	Run the simulation on a temporary, cloud-based (IaaS) computer grid

here are some quick technology tips to bear in mind as you proceed through the book:

- If you want off-the-shelf software that you can access from anywhere then choose Software as a Service; but look for solutions with comprehensive *web services interfaces* to facilitate integration with other systems.

- If you want to *customize* your software choose Platform as a Service over SaaS; but choose the solution that best matches your in-house skills, beware vendor lock-in, and consider choosing a platform that has a wide range of ready-made applications that you can plug in to yours.

- If you want complete control over your application servers use Infrastructure as a Service; but consider the *portability* of your virtual machines as you may wish to move them between clouds at some point.

- If you do not want your data to be hosted in a public cloud then use *private cloud* technologies; but choose an internal cloud management system that supports a *hybrid cloud* configuration in case you ever need to manually or dynamically increase your available computing capacity.

SUMMARY

We use the internet to transfer information between any computing devices in the world that are connected to the internet, but until recently most of the actual computing we do has been performed *locally* on the devices themselves or on corporate networks. Now, with an internet connection and cloud computing, we can interact remotely with rich and powerful, third-party, web-based systems, and use seemingly unlimited processing power as if they were already built in to our local computing devices, from anywhere at any time.

KEY SUMMARY POINTS

 The five essential characteristics of cloud computing are on-demand self-service, broad network access, resource pooling, rapid elasticity and measured service.

 Cloud computing is a paradigm shift for IT procurement because it does not involve capital investment and it is pay-per-use.

 The three main service models are Software as a Service, Platform as a Service and Infrastructure as a Service.

 The four main deployment models are public cloud, community cloud, private cloud and hybrid cloud.

 Adopting cloud computing is generally quicker and more convenient than internal solutions to many common IT problems.

QUESTION

 After reading this chapter, which service model and deployment model, if any, do you think may be the most appropriate for your business?

ACTIVITY

 Depending on your answer to the question above, view a demonstration video of a SaaS, PaaS or IaaS solution in action. Below, I will give just one example – which existed on the web at the time of writing – for each service model, but if the links do not work you can find directories of cloud providers listed in Chapter 5.

 For SaaS you could try http://www.salesforce.com/demos

 For PaaS you could try http://quickbase.intuit.com/tour

 And for IaaS you could try http://www.youtube.com/watch?v=RkVSkL76U-M

CHAPTER 2
BENEFITS OF CLOUD COMPUTING

I see, therefore, great potential for cloud computing applications to help Europe's businesses into the true ICT age, at lower costs compared to traditional IT company solutions.

Viviane Reding, EU Commissioner for Information Society and Media, November 2009

Towards the end of the first decade of the 21st century there was a worldwide financial crisis that saw businesses everywhere searching for ways to cut costs. At the same time feature-rich 'Web 2.0' technologies such as social networking websites, accessible from anywhere on different kinds of devices – including the ubiquitous iPhone from Apple – were gaining in popularity at an incredible rate, thanks in no small part to the high availability and affordability of broadband internet and mobile internet connections. So Information Technology was becoming more complex and businesses, along with the general public, were becoming ever more dependent on it; but added complexity and functionality are usually accompanied by added costs, which was not a great message for financial directors in a recession. The time was right for cloud computing, which offers some businesses considerable financial benefits, technological benefits and operational benefits, and can provide an opportunity for competitive advantage over others. As for the potential environmental benefits of cloud computing, they are debatable, as we shall see.

FINANCIAL BENEFITS

The financial benefits of cloud computing are most clear cut for public clouds, where computing resources are acquired as a utility service on demand from external providers, as described in Chapter 1. This business model means that IT can be purchased on a pay-per-use basis and treated as operational expenditure, with the reduced administration burden that comes with not having any server hardware to look after.

Pay-per-use IT

The elastic and scalable nature of cloud computing supports the unpredictable cycles of expansion and contraction that businesses go through. Public cloud customers share the cost of a multi-tenanted computing infrastructure with other customers, making their own consumption-based costs and subscription-based costs affordable and variable. Cost models vary between the three main service models: Software as a Service (SaaS), Infrastructure as a Service (IaaS) and Platform as a Service (PaaS), but the principle is the same. Your SaaS costs depend on your user numbers; your PaaS costs increase in proportion to the usage and size of the applications you develop; and your IaaS costs cover your use of servers and storage – see Chapter 5 for more details. Long-term cost savings are less likely for large enterprises as they have their own economies of scale, but many small to medium-sized businesses can benefit financially from cloud computing even in the long term.

Operational expenditure

When your business buys computing hardware it is *capital expenditure*, which increases your tax burden in the short term. Cloud computing purchases, however, are considered *operational expenditure*, because you are renting resources and accumulate no assets, so the costs can be subtracted directly from profits – an important consideration for many businesses. Moreover, building your own IT infrastructure involves significant up-front costs on hardware and software, driven by long-term planning based on forecasts of business growth and market trends, whereas a cloud computing system grows with you and, if necessary, shrinks with you. With cloud computing, hardware assets and software licences are not left unused when you downsize your business.

Reduced IT management costs

If you manage your own IT infrastructure or deploy business software applications to your employees' desktops there is an administration overhead, and this is a significant factor in the total cost of ownership. Assets have to be bought and managed, users supported and technical people employed to administrate systems and hardware. Cloud computing can reduce this overhead by offloading the problems of procuring, installing, managing and maintaining hardware (through Infrastructure as a Service); server operating systems (through Platform as a Service); and application deployment (through Software as a Service).

These overhead costs are less of an issue for organizations with large IT departments, but small to medium-sized businesses with fewer resources can certainly benefit.

TECHNOLOGICAL BENEFITS

Making the economic case for cloud computing is not simple because you need to compare accurately the total cost of owning your current systems (if any) with replacements in the cloud, and be able to predict confidently the expected return on investment (if any); but the technological benefits are clearer. Public clouds afford on-demand access to a pool of rapidly scalable computing resources from anywhere.

Rapid scalability on demand

Two of the five essential characteristics of cloud computing (see Chapter 1) are on-demand self-service and rapid elasticity, which speed up everything to do with IT provisioning. You can quickly provide new employees (temporary or permanent) with user accounts for your Software as a Service applications, and they can use any old personal computer to access it. You can develop new web-based business software applications using Platform as a Service without worrying about servers, firewalls, security or operating systems. And you can use Infrastructure as a Service to gain temporary access to seemingly unlimited computing power and data storage when you need it for as long as you need it.

Access anywhere

Because they are web-based, your access to cloud computing services does not depend on the computer you are using – all you need is a web browser; and most SaaS solutions now support popular hand-held computing devices, too, through native browsers or downloadable applications. See Figure 2.1 for an example of the Salesforce.com iPhone application in action.

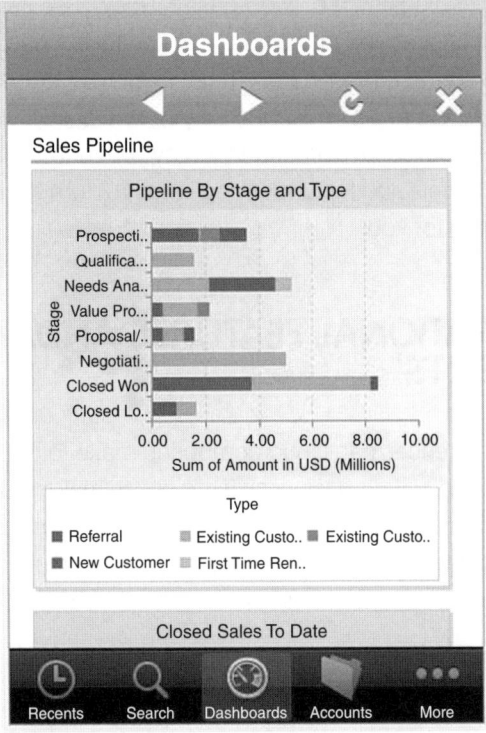

FIGURE 2.1 A screenshot of the Salesforce.com CRM iPhone application

Future proof

Assuming your cloud computing provider continues as a going concern (a risk discussed in Chapter 3) then the services they provide will be effectively future proof. With

Software as a Service (SaaS) and Platform as a Service (PaaS) you always get the latest software – updates are automatic. There are no costs for upgrading to the next version of your favourite application or development platform and it is in your supplier's interest to ensure that their systems improve and remain competitive. Moreover, because the technologies are web-based they use standard information transfer protocols, facilitating connections to other web-based software. These benefits do not apply to Infrastructure as a Service (IaaS) where any business software applications are managed by you; but your system control panels and the underlying infrastructure will be kept up-to-date for you.

OPERATIONAL FEATURES AND BENEFITS

What differences can cloud computing make to the day-to-day running of your business? Firstly it can make much of IT someone else's problem so you can focus on core business, and secondly it affords 'business beyond buildings'.

Someone else's problem

The argument for using third-party services in general is to offload non-core business activities to experts in the relevant fields. If you are busy doing what your business does best then why waste time on everyday tasks like bookkeeping or cleaning your windows when you can pay someone else to do it better and faster than you? The same goes for IT system administration, which is often a headache for businesses, especially small businesses with limited resources, but you can save precious time and avoid worries by moving some or all of your activities into a public cloud.

For example, do you really need to manage your own Microsoft Exchange e-mail server and deal with spam, viruses, databases and back-up systems internally? Do you have a disaster recovery plan should your systems fail? Do your internal IT systems depend on one or more internal staff or external IT consultants to keep them up and running?

Here is a list of common IT administration tasks you can avoid having to do yourself by using the appropriate cloud computing services:

- buying, installing, supporting and updating desktop business software on specific PCs;
- tracking hardware and software assets;
- backing up data off-site automatically and redundantly;
- setting up virtual private networks;
- securing web applications and patching web servers;
- buying and configuring server hardware that would almost certainly be underutilized;
- buying and configuring high-specification PCs when a web browser is usually all you need.

And with very little technical knowledge cloud computing enables you to perform the following tasks yourself:

- set up new user accounts for e-mail and other applications in the cloud;
- assign users to one or more role-based user groups and limit their access to IT systems according to their role;
- restore deleted or archived files and folders from back-ups;

- create or destroy a new virtual server in minutes;
- temporarily increase the performance of a web server or expand a cluster of web servers.

Business beyond buildings

Cloud computing frees you from common IT administrative tasks, but what can your business do with cloud computing technologies? Depending on any restrictions imposed by corporate governance and your organization's internal (operational) controls, here are some examples to consider:

- access your data and applications from any internet connection, regardless of the device you are using, so you can work from home or on the move in exactly the same way as you would in your office;
- avoid storing confidential business data on laptops, PCs and other devices that could be stolen;
- share documents and collaborate more easily on documents and projects with colleagues, partners and customers;
- add pre-integrated third-party applications from within your cloud or connect to applications or data sources in other clouds (LinkedIn or Facebook for example) using standard web service protocols;
- use visual web-based development tools to quickly create new web applications and document workflows that make more of your business data and speed up processes;
- run highly intensive data processing tasks on any number of duplicate virtual servers and then delete the server instances when you have your results.

ENVIRONMENTAL BENEFITS

Public cloud computing is often touted as an environmentally friendly or 'green' alternative to businesses owning their own IT infrastructures, but there are arguments for and against this claim. Sharing resources and commuting less must be a good thing, but if the enhanced technology that is available in public clouds causes businesses to use more resources together than the combined total they would have used apart then how can they be green?

Sharing resources

Some arguments for cloud computing being an energy-efficient IT solution are:

- customers share a pool of IT resources;
- suppliers are using bigger, more modern and energy-efficient data centres in purpose-built 'smart' buildings;
- increased utilization of servers due to server virtualization – vendors claim that typical server utilization rates can rise from between 5 and 15 per cent to between 60 and 80 per cent (VMWare, 2010);
- the financial incentives for cloud providers to use less energy;
- the increasing availability of follow-the-sun and follow-the-moon clouds so virtual servers and applications move between linked data centres across time zones, making more use of the combined computing resources and even taking account of the availability of energy in different geographical locations at certain times of day.

Some arguments against cloud computing technologies being green are:

- more internet traffic;
- increased data replication within public clouds;
- high demand created by new services.

According to a March 2010 Greenpeace report, *Make IT Green: Cloud Computing and its Contribution to Climate Change*, the electricity consumed by cloud computing globally will increase from 623 billion kilowatt hours in 2007 to 1,964 billion kWh by 2020 (Greenpeace, 2010).

Now, the clock cannot be turned back, the cloud computing 'genie' cannot go back into the bottle. We have to accept that internet usage will increase along with the wider adoption of cloud computing services, but the rise of social networking websites has made this an inevitable trend anyway. All we can do is to make the technology we use to provide web-based services *as green as possible*, and cloud computing providers can certainly help. Along with many leading IT firms, Google and Microsoft are members of the Climate Savers Computing Initiative (http://www.climatesaverscomputing.org/), which is a non-profit group 'dedicated to reducing the energy consumption of computers and reducing the environmental impact of new and emerging technologies', so let us hope they can rise to the significant challenge that cloud computing represents.

Reduced travel

Naturally, cloud computing means that we no longer have to travel to an office to do office work, nor do our system administrators have to go to data centres to install new servers. It is now much easier to work from home and many of us do already – in the UK, for example, at least 8 per cent of the workforce in 2005 used computers and telecommunications to work mainly from home (Ruiz and Walling, 2005). If global warming is a reality, as most of the scientists of our time agree, then I would like to think that cloud computing or 'cloud commuting' will help to make most business travel unnecessary and reduce significantly the impact of business activities on the environment, but only time will tell. According to Viviane Reading, EU Commissioner for Information Society and Media: 'If businesses in Europe were to replace only 20 per cent of all business trips by video conferencing, we could save more than 22 million tons of CO_2 per year' (Donaghue, 2009).

I first wrote about 'cloud computing commuters' in my blog post of 19 February 2009, concluding it with speculation about their possible effect on cities:

I can predict with more confidence that, although there will always be value in face-to-face meetings, there will be far less time, money and energy wasted on commuting in the decade to come. London's workforce will consist increasingly of virtual commuters, doing ever more complex business in the cloud. Whether London itself, or cities in general, will still be as important in the business world is another matter, and it may all depend on those cloud computing commuters. (Williams, 2009)

COMPETITIVE ADVANTAGE

As I mentioned at the beginning of this chapter, cloud computing first rose to prominence in the IT industry in 2008, at least with suppliers and the media, just as a financial crisis stunned the world, and I wrote about this coincidence at the time in my blog (Williams, 2008). Then in a later post I speculated on how cloud computing could give smaller companies a competitive advantage in an uncertain financial landscape:

New startups will not find investment easy to find so they will, by necessity, keep costs down and avoid capital expenditure where possible. These new companies will naturally use pay-per-use, cloud computing technologies, and their staff will more often than not be contractors, working mostly from home. With their established competitors losing money and people, clever startups have a great opportunity to gain market share quickly.

As for established companies that were around in the boom years before the credit crunch, they will have to adapt or die, and that means mimicking the business models of startups, writing off old investments and keeping their best people, even as contractors. (Williams, 2009)

Moreover, as was mentioned earlier in this chapter, enterprise-class businesses are constrained by corporate governance and internal policies so public clouds are often not a viable option; but smaller businesses usually have no such restrictions. Of course small to medium-sized businesses and enterprises are generally not direct competitors, but if there are enough new entrants of the former variety into an industry where IT-enabled systems and innovation count, they can eat significantly into an enterprise's market share. And with the capability afforded by many cloud computing platforms to quickly develop scalable and feature-rich, customer-focused web applications (and integrated online workflow processes) without having to worry about IT infrastructure, there is great potential for market disruption.

Even in more prosperous times it pays for businesses to be *agile*, to be able to respond quickly to changes in market conditions and technological developments. The *flexibility* and *scalability* that cloud computing affords levels the playing field for businesses of different sizes. Small businesses can now afford enterprise-class IT systems so big businesses had better watch out!

SUMMARY

In this chapter I described some of the benefits of cloud computing.

KEY SUMMARY POINTS

 Financial benefits include pay-per-use IT, operational expenditure and reduced IT management costs.

 Technological benefits include rapidly scalable computing on demand, access anywhere and future proofing.

 Operational benefits include fewer IT administration tasks, remote access, online collaboration and faster software development and deployment.

 There are environmental benefits from sharing resources and reduced travel, but whether cloud computing is good for the environment overall is debatable.

 Cloud computing helps small businesses compete with larger enterprises.

 And it enables businesses in general to be more agile and quicker to market.

QUESTION

After reading this chapter, which features of cloud computing do you think might benefit your business most?

ACTIVITY

Ask contacts in the same organizational sector as you if they are using cloud computing, and, if so, what are they using it for and why? And if you would rather not ask this question of your contacts then why not search online forums for your sector to see if the subject has been mentioned?

CHAPTER 3
RISKS OF CLOUD COMPUTING

People always fear change. People feared electricity when it was invented, didn't they? People feared coal; they feared gas-powered engines. There will always be ignorance, and ignorance leads to fear. But with time, people will come to accept their silicon masters.

From a *spoof interview* with Bill Gates,
Microsoft Chairman, 2000

It is amazing how this completely fake and outlandish 'quote' has spread around the internet, but I could not resist reproducing it here. It is true that the further removed we become from technology the more we initially feel the lack of control, but eventually we get used to it. Nevertheless there are genuinely good reasons why you should not take cloud computing lightly and this chapter addresses a number of risks that you should take account of before moving any of your business data or systems into a public cloud. These risks include internal security breaches; cloud security breaches; data protection risks; system outages; data loss; vendor lock-in and vendor failure. Appetites for risk vary from business to business and industry to industry but the risk calculator included at the end of this chapter should help you decide whether a particular risk is worth taking.

INTERNAL SECURITY RISKS

If your business replaces its desktop software with web-based applications, or its internal firewall-protected servers with externally hosted systems, then they become more easily accessible over the internet, which is presumably what you want, but there are associated internal security risks whether they are cloud-based or not. Rogue employees are a danger to any business on any system, and 'insider theft' accounted for 16 per cent of reported data breaches in the United States in 2008 (ITRC, 2009); but here are three scenarios that relate to web-based systems in general:

- Former employees or contractors may continue to have access to your intellectual property after they have stopped working for your organization if one or more of their user accounts have not been deactivated.

- Users may have their user names and passwords stolen by keyboard sniffing technology or professional hackers who use various techniques.

- If you use the same user name and password on multiple systems and one system is compromised, then those credentials may be used to access another system.

Now, mistakes happen, but there are ways to minimize the likelihood of internal security breaches, including internal processes, two-factor authentication and single sign-on.

Internal processes

Most businesses have checklists they use and processes they follow when employees take up or leave their employment; but the deployment of new IT systems in public clouds can outpace the development of internal security processes, especially when they can be set up by non-IT staff. Thus, whenever a new cloud-based system is introduced, checklists must be modified immediately and existing user account management processes must be followed or, if necessary, extended to encompass them. You have to ensure through good internal processes that all ex-employees' and ex-contractors' user accounts are deactivated immediately to reduce the risk of these accounts being misused or confidential data passed on to competitors. You should also ensure that your employees use strong passwords when they access any of your systems, and that they use different passwords on different systems unless *single sign-on* technology is implemented.

Two-factor authentication

User names and passwords can be guessed or stolen, along with other personal information such as your mother's maiden name or your place of birth, and so on. Thus if you really want to secure access to your cloud-based systems then two-factor authentication is a good solution. This means keeping your user name and password but adding another identifying element that is immune to online identity theft. Examples of two-factor authentication techniques are:

- asking users (when they attempt to log on) to view a group of similar images and select the one that they chose or uploaded when they registered as a user on the system;

- biometric techniques such as retinal scans or voice prints;

- comparing the 'typing rhythm' of a user with recorded patterns for that user when they enter their user credentials;

- one-time passwords generated by a small portable 'token' carried by users;

- public-key infrastructure, which involves a public and a private cryptographic key pair that is obtained and shared through a 'trusted authority';

- sending one-time passwords to users' mobile phones for them to type in after they have entered their usual credentials;

- *smart cards* that have on them a unique security grid which has characters in specific coordinates that the user can be quizzed on when logging in.

Two-factor authentication technologies are not new to cloud computing, they have been used to secure the virtual private networks of enterprises for some time, but the economies of scale afforded by public clouds have now made them affordable for small businesses.

Single sign-on

As discussed earlier, your employees may end up with user accounts on multiple cloud-based systems so password management becomes a problem, and the temptation is there to use the same password on different systems, which is a security risk. To deal with this issue of 'cloud proliferation' there are a number of commercially available federated identity (or single sign-on) services that enable users to log on to multiple clouds and internal IT systems through a single website; and some cloud service providers also allow users to log on to their systems using their credentials from other cloud services without a third party being involved.

EXTERNAL SECURITY RISKS

Data stored in public clouds can be compromised as a result of failures in a provider's security technology or its operational security practices, and this is a major risk in a multi-tenanted system where business competitors share the same IT infrastructure. If you have internal policies for information governance that encompasses security then you must ensure that your cloud provider takes security as seriously as your business – some key security questions are provided below. And it is important to be aware that you are responsible for keeping your confidential customer data safe, not your cloud provider!

Security technology failures

An example of a security technology failure in a public cloud was the bug found in Google Docs (a Software as a Service system) in March 2009 that led to a small percentage of documents being inadvertently shared with unauthorized users (Mazzon, 2009). But the fact that, at the time of writing, it was difficult to find any other significant examples, despite the large number of cloud computing providers and media attention, speaks volumes. It is in the interest of these providers to secure their systems, and they typically have far more resources to devote to the problem than their customers.

Operational security failures

An example of an operational security failure in another Software as a Service system was the Twitter hack of January 2009 where a hacker gained access to system support tools and took temporary control of the Twitter user accounts of President Barack Obama, among others (Twitter, 2009). In the Twitter example the hacker allegedly took advantage of a weak password on a support user account to gain access (Zetter, 2009). Again it is difficult to find further examples, and it is unlikely that providers of more business-critical cloud-based systems would be so careless in their use of passwords. But cloud providers are well aware that the most common fear about cloud computing, particularly in public clouds, is over security and a number of them have joined forces to form the *Cloud Security Alliance*, a non-profit organization that promotes best practices and provides comprehensive (and free) cloud security guidance documents at http://www.cloudsecurityalliance.org/.

Key security questions

Chapter 5 provides further guidance on choosing suppliers, but here are some key questions to ask them about the security of their systems with regards to their technologies and operations:

- Are security tests an integral part of their software development cycle?

- Are security issues specifically addressed in technical training programmes?
- Are non-technical employees made aware of security issues when they are trained?
- Are third-party security audits performed, and, if so, by whom, how thorough and how often?
- What operational policies and controls are in place, what do they cover and are they assessed by third parties?

DATA PROTECTION RISKS

If a security breach results in sensitive customer details being stolen your business may be prosecuted by national authorities, penalized by standards bodies or sued by your customers. In the UK the Information Commissioner's Office is using existing laws such as the Data Protection Act to take action against offending organizations if any security breaches are shown to be due to inadequate controls. And, in the financial industry, regulations and standards are being imposed on organizations compelling them to use effective security controls, and in some cases specifying the type of controls to use. For example, the Payment Card Industry Data Security Standards (PCI DSS) specify two-factor authentication 'for remote access for all employees, administrators, and third parties'.

The main questions that need to be answered by organizations that have to comply with data protection regulations are:

- What information is stored on a system?
- Where is the information stored?

- Who can access the system?
- What can they access?
- Is the access appropriate?

Now, cloud computing providers can certainly tell you *what* information is stored on their systems, but *where* the information is stored is less certain because of the distributed and virtualized nature of public clouds. If this is an issue you will have to ensure that the provider you use is able and willing to work with you to provide, and prove, any data location restrictions you may have. As for the 'who', 'what' and 'why' questions about system access, in order to comply with data protection regulations, you may have to find out who the system and application administrators are; how they access the systems; and the policies that dictate how administrative security permissions are granted. The provider may also need to prove they can provide you with an audit trail based on detailed system access logs, if required.

As a minimum precaution, if your business has personal data records that are stored and moved around public clouds that cross international boundaries then you should ensure that your cloud provider – and any country where your data may be stored – adheres to the data protection principles contained in the *Safe Harbour* arrangement between the European Commission and the US Department of Commerce (http://epic.org/privacy/intl/EP_SH_resolution_0700.html).

At the dawn of the cloud computing era there were very few public cloud solutions that offered this level of data protection, but as the technologies mature they may become more standards-compliant. In the meantime you may have to rely on the wording in service contracts to assist you with cloud compliance (see Chapter 5).

CLOUD OUTAGES

There have been many high-profile outages in public clouds, including those provided by, perhaps, the four most famous names in cloud computing – Amazon, Google, Microsoft and Salesforce.com. Table 3.1 below, which I compiled from numerous news reports, records at least 23 cases in two years from these four companies (Williams, 2010). Note that in some cases the outages were partial and did not affect all users, but if your company was affected this would be no consolation to you.

TABLE 3.1 Reported outages in Amazon, Google, Microsoft and Salesforce.com public clouds in 2008 and 2009

Service outage	Date	Duration
Amazon S3	15 Feb 2008	4 hours
Amazon EC2	7 Apr 2008	1 hour
Amazon S3	20 Jul 2008	8.5 hours
Amazon EC2	11 Jun 2009	7 hours
Amazon EC2	9 Dec 2009	1 to 5 hours
Google App Engine	17 Jun 2008	7 hours
Google Gmail	16 Jul 2008	1.5 hours
Google Apps & Gmail	6 Aug 2008	about 15 hours
Google Gmail	11 Aug 2008	1.5 hours
Google Gmail	15 Aug 2008	more than 24 hours

TABLE 3.1 *Continued*

Service outage	Date	Duration
Google Gmail	16 Oct 2008	30 hours
Google Gmail	24 Feb 2009	2.5 hours
Google Gmail	9 Mar 2009	up to 22 hours
Google network	14 May 2009	2 hours
Google App Engine	2 Jul 2009	6 hours
Google Gmail	1 Sep 2009	2 hours
Google Gmail	24 Sep 2009	2.5 hours
Microsoft Windows Live	26 Feb 2008	About 6 hours
Microsoft Hotmail	12 Mar 2009	5 hours
Microsoft Azure	13 Mar 2009	22 hours
Microsoft Sidekick	4 Oct 2009	6 days + total loss of contact data
Salesforce.com	11 Feb 2008	6 hours
Salesforce.com	6 Jan 2009	1 hour

If outages would severely affect your business and you are confident your internal IT infrastructure is more reliable than public cloud services then it may be advisable to only move non-critical business applications into the cloud. But are your internal IT infrastructures really more reliable than public clouds? According to IDC, the average mid-size company experiences 16 to 20 business hours of network, system or application downtime each year, which equates to 99.8 per cent availability (Boggs *et al*, 2009), while service providers such as Amazon, Google, Microsoft and Salesforce.com aim to provide at least 99.9 per cent availability and deliver on that promise for the most part (see again Table 3.1). Even with all the problems Google experienced with its Gmail service in 2008, which mainly affected a 'small number of users', it was still available at least 99.2 per cent of the time for *all users*, and they guarantee at least 99.9 per cent availability for Google Apps Premier Edition.

DATA LOSS

A major argument for placing computing resources into a public cloud is to remove a troublesome burden for your business and let someone else worry about data back-ups and failover systems. But unless your cloud computing provider has completely redundant systems in multiple geographical locations and can explain exactly how they recover from disasters, with evidence of successful test recoveries, then you should still worry. One example of complete data loss was in October 2009 when many T-Mobile Sidekick users lost their contacts data that were stored in a cloud provided by Microsoft's Danger unit (Fried, 2009). Another example was in September 2007 when the deployment of new monitoring software caused some Amazon EC2 virtual machine instances to be deleted, affecting a small number of Amazon customers (Miller, 2007).

So what can you do to prevent data loss in public clouds? One solution is to take a hybrid approach where only non-critical business applications and data are stored in public clouds. Another solution is to use a secondary public cloud as a back-up for your primary public cloud, assuming you are not locked in to a particular technology

– see next section. But if you do decide to put critical business data in a public cloud then it is your responsibility to ensure that your provider's disaster recovery processes are tried and tested. Your business can survive occasional system outages but very few businesses survive the loss of their data. See Chapter 5 for tips on how to select a supplier.

VENDOR LOCK-IN

A common fear among potential public cloud customers is being locked into a particular vendor's cloud. If you use Software as a Service (SaaS) can you extract your data or transfer data between applications in different clouds in real-time if required? If you use Platform as a Service are you able to move your software applications and business logic to another cloud or a private cloud? And with Infrastructure as a Service are you able to move your virtual servers between clouds? Well, the first SaaS applications were effectively 'walled gardens', but with the rise of cloud computing have come proposals from industry consortia and standards organizations on how clouds may interoperate so the walls are slowly coming down.

Some examples of cloud interoperability proposals are listed below:

- The Cloud Computing Interoperability Forum (CCIF – http://www.cloudforum.org/) aims to create 'a common agreed-upon framework/ontology that enables the ability of two or more cloud platforms to exchange information in [a] unified manner'.

- The Distributed Management Task Force's Open Cloud Standards Incubator (http://www.dmtf.org/about/cloud-incubator) focuses on 'standardizing interactions between cloud environments by developing cloud resource management protocols, packaging formats and security mechanisms to facilitate interoperability'.

● The Open Cloud Manifesto (http://www. opencloudmanifesto.org/) is an attempt to establish 'a core set of principles to ensure that organizations will have freedom of choice, flexibility, and openness as they take advantage of cloud computing'. The manifesto is supported by Cisco, IBM, RackSpace, Red Hat, Sun Microsystems, VMWare and many more cloud providers, big and small.

● The Open Grid Forum's Open Cloud Computing Interface Working Group (http://www.occi-wg.org/) aims to 'deliver an API specification for remote management of cloud computing infrastructure, allowing for the development of interoperable tools for common tasks including deployment, autonomic scaling and monitoring'.

Cloud computing providers are now under pressure to be interoperable, but it is worth keeping the *exit door* in view whenever you enter a public cloud. One Platform as a Service provider that makes it particularly easy to move applications away from its cloud is Zoho with their Zoho Creator (http://creator.zoho.com). With Zoho Creator you can develop simple database applications, download them as a zip file and then upload them into Google's cloud. As for *private clouds*, you can choose between proprietary cloud management software and open-source software, if vendor lock-in is a consideration; but make sure that the software supports interoperability, too, so you can move services into public clouds if required.

VENDOR FAILURE

What happens if your cloud provider goes out of business or is acquired by a competitor? In February 2009, Coghead, a Platform as a Service provider, informed their customers that they had nine weeks to find a new home for their software applications as, 'due to the impact of economic challenges', they had discontinued operations (Austin, 2009). And around the same time, and for the same reasons, I had to inform the customers of Extrasys, a Software as a Service Provider, that our failing business had been sold to another provider of Hosted Desktops. In the case of Coghead the affected customers were locked in to a platform and had a lot of work to do to migrate their software applications, whereas in Extrasys's case the platform was Microsoft Windows so the migration to the new provider's infrastructure was relatively painless for our customers (see the Department 83 case study in Chapter 4); but in both cases the customers were taken by surprise. As a general rule, then, do not place critical business systems or data into a public cloud unless the provider is financially stable and you have a reliable exit plan that you can execute quickly.

RISK CALCULATOR

The appetite for risk varies from business to business and from industry to industry, but there is perhaps one golden rule when considering a cloud service: it is your responsibility to ensure that the service provider can look after your data and systems at least as well as you can.

Regardless of the potential benefits and cost savings that may be had with a particular service you must first attempt to calculate the risk associated with that service before making a decision about using it for a particular project. Firstly, how forthcoming is the provider regarding their systems and operations, do they address satisfactorily the risks identified in this chapter, and are they inspected regularly and thoroughly by independent specialists? Secondly, how critical is your project to your business and how sensitive is any data that may be stored or processed in the cloud? These two questions can be represented, respectively, as *provider transparency* and *business importance* in a simple risk calculator represented by a quadrant chart – see Figure 3.1.

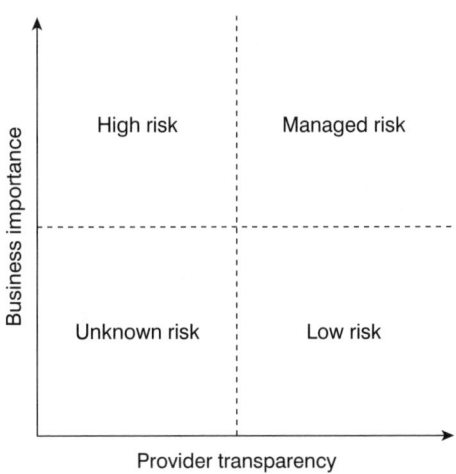

FIGURE 3.1 A simple risk calculator for cloud computing

If your project has low business importance then you may decide to spend little time performing due diligence checks, leaving you with *unknown risk*, which may eventually become a problem if your project is a success and its importance increases; but if you do perform adequate checks of provider transparency then your 'unimportant' cloud use has *low risk*, which is the safest position to be in. If, however, your project has high business importance then you will have *high risk*, too, if you are not assured of provider transparency, but *managed risk* if you do your due diligence.

SUMMARY

In this chapter we have examined some of the most common risks associated with public clouds. Cloud computing services are maturing at a rapid rate and solutions are being developed to solve most of the potential problems identified in this chapter, but, in the end, you are entrusting your data and applications to a third party and it is up to you to gauge whether they are worthy of your trust.

KEY SUMMARY POINTS

 Cloud computing risks include internal security breaches; cloud security breaches; data protection risks; system outages; data loss; vendor lock-in and vendor failure.

 You can reduce your internal risks through user account management processes and security technologies such as two-factor authentication and single sign-on.

 You can you reduce your external risks by choosing providers that have good answers to your questions on security, data protection and cloud interoperability.

 You can further reduce your risks if you choose projects that are not business-critical and you store only non-sensitive data in public clouds.

QUESTION

After reading this chapter, which of the well-known risks of cloud computing described above are most relevant to your business, and are there any other risks that you can think of?

ACTIVITY

E-mail relevant colleagues or review relevant internal documentation to find out if your internal processes and information governance would need to be adapted to accommodate cloud computing.

CHAPTER 4
CASE STUDIES

It would appear that we have reached the limits of what it is possible to achieve with computer technology, although one should be careful with such statements, as they tend to sound pretty silly in five years.

John Von Neumann, mathematician and
pioneering computer scientist, 1949

Von Neumann, genius though he was, would surely be amazed at what we are doing with computers today! This chapter includes two exclusive cloud computing case studies – one from a small company, Department 83, and one long case study from a large organization, the Open University – to illustrate the fact that *size matters* when it comes to making important decisions about cloud computing. But, before I get to the exclusive case studies, I have reproduced, in summary form, a number of other examples of success stories for organizations in the cloud, which I sourced from the web. These case studies cover the three cloud computing service models: Software as a Service (SaaS), Platform as a Service (PaaS) and Infrastructure as a Service (IaaS).

To demonstrate the broad appeal of cloud computing, and to help you find a case study you can relate to in this chapter, I have listed below the sectors that are covered by these SaaS, PaaS and IaaS case studies:

- **Charity** – Oxfam America (PaaS);
- **Education** – The Open University (SaaS);
- **Financial services** – SunTrust Bank (SaaS);
- **Media** – The Guardian Media Group (SaaS); and the *New York Times* (IaaS);
- **Professional services** – Department 83 (SaaS);
- **Retail** – Alliance Boots (SaaS);
- **Software services** – LinkedIn (IaaS); and FinancialForce.com (PaaS).

SAAS CASE STUDIES

I have reproduced here case studies from customers of two of the most famous Software as a Service (SaaS) providers – Google and Salesforce.com – along with a case study from Alliance Boots, a customer of Huddle, a smaller provider that focuses on providing a single specialized SaaS product to a growing customer base. The Google customer story is on The Guardian Media Group who switched from Microsoft Office to Google Apps. The SunTrust Banks (Salesforce.com) case study shows that even some financial services companies are sufficiently confident that their data is safe in trusted public clouds. And to prove that public cloud providers really believe in cloud computing there is a brief case study on how Google made use of the Salesforce.com public cloud.

Alliance Boots

Alliance Boots, the international, pharmacy-led health and beauty group which operates Boots high street stores in the UK, has transformed key aspects of its business through the use of Huddle (http://www.huddle.net/) online SaaS tools for projects and collaboration. The implementation in August 2008 comprised 300 users within Boots' support offices (Huddle, 2008). The tool was required by Boots to ensure the customer was at the heart of all decision-making processes from trading and ranging decisions through to creation of store layouts and marketing activities. They chose Huddle because it was a 'credible' off-the-shelf solution for online collaboration that was quick to implement.

At first Huddle was primarily used for internal communication and collaboration, but Boots went on to make some of its tender process documents available on Huddle to be shared externally with potential business partners. A key concern for Boots was data security so internal data, including customer data from Boots Advantage loyalty cards, was restricted to certain IP addresses only.

Huddle has radically changed the way our key business units operate, in that our Customer Insight material is now accessible by all teams all over the world via a simple web browser without having to download anything onto their individual computers. Our business units consult with each other more efficiently through Huddle. The key benefit is that material now flows freely throughout the business to support critical business decisions.

The main change in working practices, and a continual challenge, is to drive the team to continually upload documents and refer users onto Huddle rather than clog up e-mail systems and shared networks. When material is uploaded and shared, there is no question about where the latest, most current version resides, so we don't waste time looking for it or waiting for our beleaguered e-mail server to download it.

Now, when people come to us with queries, in nine times out of 10, they have already looked up background research on the Huddle workspace, so less of our time is wasted explaining things.

Martin Duffy, contracts manager
in Boots' Customer Insights team

SunTrust Banks, Inc

In 2004 one of the largest banks in the United States, SunTrust Banks, Inc, saw a need to differentiate itself by providing a personalized, localized service to its clients while improving the productivity of its relationship managers and maximizing cross-selling opportunities among its five lines of business. With numerous systems running in the background, SunTrust found it difficult to get a consistent, comprehensive view of client data. Moreover, the sales methodology in which SunTrust had invested was not supported by its tools. Given the intensely competitive nature of the banking industry, SunTrust sought to deploy a Customer Relationship Management (CRM) system *quickly*, and Salesforce.com fitted the bill (Salesforce.com, 2004).

We needed sales automation, we needed it integrated with key legacy systems, and we needed it yesterday. With the help of the [Salesforce.com] professional services team, we were ready to begin training our people in 77 days; in 90 days the 110-person pilot was up and running.

Jim Wilson, group vice president of delivery services and
planning, SunTrust Banks, Inc

To assess the risk of storing data in an external system, SunTrust assembled a team to ensure that Salesforce. com could meet its standards for security, performance and availability. Other must-have capabilities included customization and integration with other systems, and Salesforce.com ticked these boxes, too.

SunTrust deployed the CRM in two stages to eventually reach 2,700 users in its Commercial Banking and Business Banking divisions. With help from Salesforce.com consultants, SunTrust integrated the CRM with a proprietary data warehouse that serves as an integration hub for its other systems, affording a complete view of customers and relationships across the business, and they customized the CRM to drive its sales methodology. Headline results for the deployment were:

- The project was delivered on time and $175,000 under budget.

- After two years of using the CRM, SunTrust experienced significant return on investment including a 67 per cent increase in capital market fees and a 29 per cent increase in treasury fees year over year.

- In two years the company also saw a 31 per cent increase in wealth management referrals and a 5 per cent increase in loan referrals.

- SunTrust achieved a marked increase in lead relationships, achieving the highest in the industry.

- Improved employee productivity resulted in thousands of additional sales opportunities that yielded millions in revenue.

- The ramp-up time for new relationship managers was reduced from months to days.

- The time relationship managers spent preparing for sales meetings was cut by more than half.

- SunTrust enhanced its corporate culture by providing the tools to develop client relationships and foster increased internal information sharing and accountability.

The Guardian Media Group

In August 2008 the Guardian Media Group (GMG) began its switch from Lotus Notes e-mail and Microsoft Office applications to Google Apps, and within six months 300 Google sites had been set up for internal collaborations and 70 per cent of users had accessed their accounts (Robinson, 2009). According to GMG's technology director Andy Beale, they wanted a system that would address their needs for a more productive and collaborative workplace, and Google was a model their people were familiar with. 'The way we were doing it before pretty much summed up as word attachments in e-mail,' he said (Kobie, 2009). The benefits they experienced were:

- no official training was required as many staff were already familiar with Google Docs and Gmail;
- the only implementation tasks were to do with migrating e-mail accounts;
- fewer calls to the helpdesk about e-mail issues after switching from Lotus Notes;
- users are now using Google Postini to manage their own e-mail blacklists and retrieve messages, which used to require an IT administrator's involvement;
- there were quick savings to be made on Lotus licence costs.

The decision to switch to Software as a Service (SaaS) and place their data in a public cloud was not taken lightly by

GMG and they carried out a risk assessment before proceeding. Aside from potential security risks there were major concerns about sensitive information being stored in the United States where the Patriot Act allows the government to inspect any data stored on its shores, so they had to be confident that Google's systems gave them full control of their information, including setting access permissions and deleting data.

> *Google Apps forms a major part of our strategic IT objectives for the business. It facilitates a new way of working for our staff and cuts out a lot of the administrative and functional difficulties most traditional IT departments have to deal with.*
> Andy Beale, technology director,
> Guardian Media Group

Google and Salesforce.com

Google Enterprise, which offers enterprise solutions to organizations of all sizes, used to store customer data in multiple systems, which made it difficult for them to view their total sales pipeline. They chose the Salesforce.com CRM because it was a system that they could customize and integrate with Google Apps and other Google products (Salesforce.com, 2007). Users can now communicate and collaborate with Gmail, Google Calendar, Google Talk, Google Sites and Google Docs seamlessly within Salesforce CRM. The company subsequently acquired Postini, an e-mail services company, and dMarc Broadcasting, who were both customers of Salesforce.com, too, which facilitated the integration of their sales people. And Google did not keep their integration work to themselves; other Salesforce.com customers can also benefit from using the two clouds in tandem (McMullan, 2008).

*With Salesforce CRM and Google Apps, we have one
seamless experience. Our sales teams can collaborate,
put together a presentation, and deliver in a timely and
effective manner.*

Google (Salesforce.com, 2007)

PAAS CASE STUDIES

Software as a Service gives you a ready-made solution to a
common problem, Infrastructure as a Service provides you
with a blank canvas, but Platform as a Service (PaaS) gives
you a powerful set of software development tools and, in
many cases, a market for distributing your software. One of
the most feature-rich platforms is Force.com so it would be
remiss of me to not to reproduce one of their case studies
(FinancialForce.com) here, but there are many alternative
platforms, including Zoho Creator, which features in the
second PaaS case study below (Oxfam America).

FinancialForce.com

FinancialForce Accounting (http://www.financialforce.com/)
was the first international Software as a Service accounting
system developed on Salesforce.com's Platform as a
Service system, Force.com. FinancialForce.com (originally
called CODA 2go) was built by CODA Ltd who had
30 years' experience with on-premise financial software,
but realized that the future of software is on demand and
in the cloud.

After consulting Salesforce.com engineers, CODA
began with a pilot project using simulated data from a
fictional but realistic target customer: a mid-size business
with multiple offices managing a sizeable inventory. They

made particular use of two standard features of the Force.com platform – reporting and workflow – and they integrated their software with the core Salesforce.com CRM so that Salesforce.com customers can add accounting software to their systems with a click of a button. By using Force.com, CODA saved an estimated two years of development work while opening new market opportunities (Salesforce.com, 2008).

> *On-demand solutions are not only growing in popularity, but – as Salesforce.com has proven – can have broad market penetration. It became clear to us that we needed to be on an on-demand platform, and that ultimately meant building on Force.com.*
>
> Liz Schofield, group marketing manager, CODA

Oxfam America

In 2007, Oxfam America, an international relief and development organization, were campaigning to reform the 2007 Farm Bill. They needed to set up an affordable, password-protected, web-based data collection tool to collaborate with allies, lead organizers and activists. After ruling out Microsoft Access and spending some time researching alternative database tools, Lindsay Shade, online communications coordinator of Oxfam, found Zoho Creator. Using Zoho Creator, Oxfam were able to track and report on their lobbying efforts leading up to the House campaign; and the reports were crucial to developing and adjusting their campaign strategy, enhancing their ability to identify policy makers who might be on the cusp of supporting their reform (Zoho, 2007).

> *If we did not have access to Zoho Creator, we probably would have taken much longer to launch/implement the data-*

collection tools we needed and would not have been able to collect much of the valuable information that we used to inform our campaign strategy during the run-up to the House vote on the 2007 Farm Bill. In fact it probably would have taken several weeks longer, and that means we would have had no lobby information to use before the House vote. We also continued to make use of Zoho Creator to impact the Senate vote.

Lindsay Shade, online communications coordinator of Oxfam

IAAS CASE STUDIES

Perhaps the first high-profile example of what can be done with Infrastructure as a Service (IaaS) is the story of a particularly innovative developer at the *New York Times* so I will retell the tale here, along with a less famous but equally impressive one from LinkedIn.

The New York Times

In November 2007 Derek Gottfrid, a developer from the *New York Times*, used Amazon Web Services and a great deal of technical skill to solve a difficult problem for his employers (Gottfrid, 2007). The newspaper wanted to make all its public domain articles from 1851–1922 available on the web free of charge, but the articles were broken up into individual images scanned from the original paper that had to be pieced together. This could be done dynamically on a website for any article, but if the website proved popular then the web server could soon be overloaded with processes and grind to a halt. If there were static PDF copies of the articles to download then the website would not have to work anywhere near as hard, but there were 11 million articles to process and a tight and inflexible deadline to meet. Gottfrid's solution was to use open-source tools to process four terabytes of image data in parallel on 100 Amazon Elastic Compute Cloud (EC2) virtual machines, storing the resulting 1.5 terabytes of articles in Amazon's cloud using the Simple Storage Service (S3). The whole process took just under 24 hours and cost $240, paid for on the newspaper's company credit card; the 100 EC2 instances had done their job and were deleted.

LinkedIn

In 2007, LinkedIn, a Software as a Service business networking tool, created and launched Bumper Sticker, a very successful Facebook application hosted on Joyent's Infrastructure as a Service (http://www.joyent.com). Bumper Sticker is a viral media-sharing application that allows users to express their individuality by sticking small virtual stickers on Facebook profiles. The Joyent cloud enabled Bumper Sticker to grow to more than 1 billion page views a month within two months after launch (Hoff, 2008; Joyent, 2008). LinkedIn also uses Joyent infrastructure to operate several LinkedIn sub-domains including mobile.linkedin.com, and in October 2009 they launched their own open Platform as a Service (http://developer.linkedin.com/), further confirming their public cloud presence.

SIZE MATTERS IN THE CLOUD

Often, small businesses that adopt cloud computing do so in a big way because it gives them scalable, enterprise-level IT services for relatively low and predictable costs. Large organizations, however, are burdened with legacy systems and security worries so they are more likely to take 'baby steps' into public clouds. The following two case studies are good examples of these differences between small companies and large enterprises. The first case study tells the story of an early adopter, Department 83, who now run their *whole business* in a public cloud, while the second is about the Open University, who, at the time of writing, were on the verge of moving certain, *non-critical* IT functions into the cloud.

Department 83

I interviewed Lucy Handley for this book on 15 January 2010. Handley is the founder and managing director of Department 83, a strategic communications results consultancy, established in 2002, that specializes in developing and implementing targeted speaker programmes for corporate clients worldwide. At the time of writing, Department 83 had five employees at their Wiltshire office in the UK and a network of freelancers working on various projects who were based elsewhere in the UK and Europe. In 2006 they signed a contract with Extrasys (http://www.extrasys.com/) to provide them with Hosted Desktops with online data storage, Microsoft Office, e-mail and other applications on a *per user per month* subscription basis.

According to Handley, before Department 83 discovered Extrasys, their IT systems were 'cobbled together' and 'it was a nightmare'. Handley provided the following details of their IT problems:

- they had freelancers out in the field that could not access the Department 83 server and were using their own e-mail accounts – so e-mail messages 'invariably went astray';

- information often had to be posted to these freelancers, which caused delays and inhibited business growth;
- business files and e-mails were backed up to CD once a week;
- they were inundated with spam e-mail.

Handley 'used to have panic attacks at 3 o'clock in the morning' wondering whether she had remembered the weekly backups. So when she saw the Extrasys desktop for the first time she was 'absolutely amazed', and said, 'I want one of those!' The benefits for Department 83, according to Handley, were:

- it enabled their small company to work with large organizations at the same level;
- their freelancers could access and edit company e-mail and documents from anywhere;
- they could increase or decrease user numbers when required;
- reduction in spam e-mails;
- no worries about backing up data;
- there was no disruption in business if any of their office-based staff had to work remotely for an extended period, which was 'a huge value-add', said Handley.

Regarding the security of their data, Handley had this to say:

Here was a company who had invested in the technology to make sure that the data they were going to hold for us was going to be looked after; it was going to be secure and it was going to be backed up, and I felt very confident about it.

So, no, I had no issues at all about it and neither did any of the team. I think we were all just incredibly relieved to be able to get on with focusing on our clients rather than all our IT hiccups.

Even after more than three years using Extrasys-hosted desktops, and following two data centre migrations and the sale of the Extrasys business, Department 83 'haven't really had any bad experiences', said Handley, who later went on to say: 'the actual speed is just as good as if it was working purely from a computer desktop; so we certainly can't fault it; *we would certainly never go back*.'

The Open University

The Open University (OU) was established in 1969 and remains the United Kingdom's only university dedicated to distance learning. The OU has around 150,000 undergraduate students and more than 30,000 postgraduate students. I interviewed Niall Sclater, director of learning innovation for the Open University, on 7 January 2010 to find out what their plans were for utilizing cloud computing. Sclater revealed that, although he has been tasked with investigating cloud computing in general, the OU's '*primary need* was for e-mail for students'.

The OU has been using a system called FirstClass for discussion forums and e-mail. 'It's very much embedded in the organization's culture and has been used for over a decade for students and associate lecturers,' said Sclater. 'It's a client-based system although there is a web version of it. A decision was taken to decommission FirstClass and try and rationalize various systems into our Virtual Learning Environment, which is based on Moodle,' he said, but Moodle does not handle e-mail so they needed another solution.

The two *cloud-based* solutions that Sclater considered were Google Apps for Education and Microsoft Live@edu. 'Microsoft and Google offer a very attractive solution for universities where they provide student e-mail (and staff e-mail if you want it) plus a whole host of other services for a specified period with a service level agreement,' he explained. The 'other services' afford contact management; instant messaging; calendaring; storing and sharing of files in any format; and Google Apps also affords online editing of documents, spreadsheets and presentations. 'Those are all things that the virtual learning environment doesn't provide,' said Sclater, 'so we see this as a great opportunity to expand our offering to students without too much work on our side to develop or even host these systems or maintain them.'

'So you can see more and more functionality that is now hosted by institutions migrating to the cloud,' said Sclater. 'E-mail is a primary example where it doesn't really make sense to host it yourselves if you can get someone to do it for free. Perhaps there'll be a cost for this long term, and that's something we'll have to stay on top of, but why would we bother hosting these services ourselves when we've got a robust service hosted by people who are experts and can deal with the spam management, for example? And scalability is an issue and student numbers may go up or down but not having to worry about that is obviously one of the key benefits of cloud computing.'

Of course moving systems into the cloud is not a decision to be taken lightly and these were the main concerns that Sclater recalled:

- **Data protection** was 'one of the biggest concerns', but the OU has 'guarantees from both those companies that they will host our data in the

European Union or the States under "Safe Harbour" legislation,' said Sclater.

- **Robustness of service** is 'an often expressed concern – what happens if it goes down?' But Sclater argued that the OU 'have problems with that internally and they are aiming to have a certain level of uptime (99.5 per cent) for their services, and they often don't manage to do that, whereas these companies do.'

- **Technology changes** may cause problems if a feature is removed or changed, or a new one is added, because the OU helpdesk would have to deal with it and course documentation may become out of date.

- **Negative publicity** for their supplier (Microsoft or Google) could be a problem because of the 'joint branding'.

- **Advertisements** placed on alumni user accounts may also make 'the systems become less pleasant' and 'less attractive' for them, said Sclater, but, crucially, advertisements will not be targeted at current students or staff.

- **Future charges** for the *currently free* services are a financial risk, but they have a four-year contract and they will be given a year's advance warning of any plans to charge educational institutions.

- **Vendor lock-in** is a potential risk, too, because, as Sclater explained, 'it is very difficult not to embed particular tools into course guides.'

- **Data loss** is another potential risk, but if the OU were to implement backups they would be 'almost defeating the whole objective of going into the cloud' so they will rely on the supplier to look after student data.

- **Security** is also a concern for the OU, however. Microsoft and Google 'have got more resources to have more secure systems than we have overall,' reasoned Sclater.

Rolling out the new SaaS system to thousands of students may take up to six months and will involve the following:

- **Keeping FirstClass running** during the transition period and deciding when to switch it off.

- **Communication** – Sclater revealed that 'there is lots of uncertainty around and people are very keen to know what is happening about e-mail in particular, and we'll have to work with stakeholders and make sure we communicate adequately to them the stages.'

- **Integration** with Moodle is one issue – the OU's online authentication system is supported by both suppliers so user accounts will have 'single sign-on', but there may also be some integration work to be done on the Moodle user interface.

- Optionally **phasing in features** would probably reduce helpdesk calls but might also make students 'think they were getting a raw deal,' fears Sclater.

- **Developing policies** for deleting user accounts, etc.

Students will gain most from the new system, Sclater predicted, because it would 'make it easier for them to communicate with their tutor group on their course, for example, and have an opportunity to instant message with those students or share documents with them. So I think the advantages are much more to the student than to us as an institution. I can't see us benefitting that much from this apart from saving a bit of costs on the e-mail hosting side.'

There were no plans at the time to move staff e-mail accounts into the cloud, but 'Anything's possible,' said Sclater, 'and I think it would be very useful for us to dip our toes in the water with this initial solution for students; see how we get on and then you could well see us, within a couple of years, re-evaluating our internal hosting of Exchange and potentially shifting everyone to the cloud.' Sclater also expects that 'learning management systems, VLEs, will migrate increasingly to the cloud' in the future. 'With these cloud-based systems,' he said, 'you can have an SLA with one particular organization, you can control it very much more, you can ensure certainly that the accessibility is there, for example, and that things aren't changing too rapidly; and that makes it much more feasible for educational institutions to go with than pointing students to a set of disparate online tools hosted by different providers.'

In the end, after a careful evaluation, Sclater announced on his blog the Open University's decision to *adopt Google Apps for Education* (Sclater, 2010). He later provided me with three reasons why they chose Google Apps:

- It affords offline working using Google Gears/ HTML5;
- Group collaboration is easier;
- It is easier to set up.

SUMMARY

This chapter presented a number of case studies for the three main cloud computing service models, including two case studies that are exclusive to this book. The fact that Google are confident enough to place their sales data in another provider's cloud speaks volumes to me.

KEY SUMMARY POINTS

 The benefits of cloud computing demonstrated in these case studies include fast deployment; increased productivity; reduced IT administration; online collaboration; cost savings; scalability; disaster recovery; and return on investment.

 Larger organizations were found to be more concerned about security and data protection in public clouds than smaller organizations, and they were very thorough in their due diligence.

QUESTION

 After reading this chapter do you think that using a cloud service would be more likely to relieve your IT management burden, enhance your business, or create new issues for you to worry about?

ACTIVITY

 Search the internet and see if you can find a cloud computing case study for your organizational sector.

CHAPTER 5
CHOOSING
A PROVIDER

The main attraction of the cloud to investors and entrepreneurs
is the idea of making money from you, on a recurring,
perpetual basis, for something you currently get for a flat rate
or for free without having to give up the money or privacy that
cloud companies hope to leverage into fortunes.

Cory Doctorow, writing for the *Guardian* newspaper,
September 2009

This quote from Doctorow (2009), one of my favourite
science fiction writers, caused quite a storm in the IT community at the time; but public cloud providers are, of course,
in the business to make money so it is worth keeping that
obvious point in mind. If after reading the previous chapters
on the risks and benefits of cloud computing you are still
interested in its potential for your business then this chapter
will help you to find potential providers and arm you with the
right questions to ask. Things to consider when you compare providers include their client references; service level
agreements; service costs; and processes and practices.

THE CROWDED CLOUD MARKETPLACE

There is now a huge range of cloud computing providers to choose from and it is quite a task to list and categorize these providers. Figure 5.1 provides a visual map of example cloud vendors that were around in 2010, which was inspired by Peter Laird's 'Cloud Vendor Taxonomy, May 2009' (Laird, 2009). The figure serves only to illustrate the breadth and depth of the cloud computing market; it is by no means comprehensive, nor does it represent a completely accurate indication of which providers were most popular at the time. Fortunately, however, there are a number of web directories to help us find providers of Software, Platform and Infrastructure as a service.

How to find SaaS providers

If Software as a Service (SaaS) looks like the right option for you then there is an independent directory of SaaS providers at http://www.saas-showplace.com/ where you can search for providers by industry sector or application category – see Figure 5.2. Other online directories include GetApp.com (http://www.getapp.com/) and SaaS Directory (http://www.saasdir.com/). And last, but not least, there is the Cloudbook.net directory of application (SaaS) providers (http://www.cloudbook.net/products-applications), which is broken down into the following functional categories:

- Collaboration (http://www.cloudbook.net/saas-collaboration);
- Sales (http://www.cloudbook.net/saas-sales);
- Data & Analytics (http://www.cloudbook.net/saas-data);

FIGURE 5.1 A visual map of example cloud providers

- Service & Support (http://www.cloudbook.net/saas-service);
- Operations (http://www.cloudbook.net/saas-operations);
- Office & Communications (http://www.cloudbook.net/saas-office);
- Marketing (http://www.cloudbook.net/saas-marketing);
- Financial (http://www.cloudbook.net/saas-financial);
- Human Resources (http://www.cloudbook.net/saas-hr);
- Vertical (http://www.cloudbook.net/saas-vertical).

SaaS Showplace®

The Software-as-a-Service & Cloud Computing Resource Center

Software-as-a-Service Providers By Application Category

There is a rapidly growing number of SaaS providers addressing nearly every business and IT application need. Select a specific application category below to find our latest listing of SaaS providers offering 'on-demand' software solutions in that area.

Click here if you'd like help selecting the best SaaS provider to meet your business and IT requirements.

Click here if you are a SaaS provider and would like to be added to our directory.

Click here if you'd like to update your company's Quick Summary Profile.

Home

About Us

SaaS Provider Directory

SaaS Marketplace

SaaS Insights

SaaS Industry News

SaaS Industry Events

Best of Showplace Awards

Best Practices Portal

Sponsorship Opportunities

Feedback/Contact Information

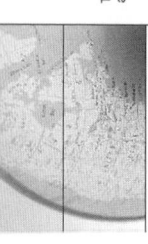

Maps

-- Select Application --

-- Select Application --
Accounting/Financial
Asset Management
Business Intelligence
Business Process Management
Call Center
Channel Management
Collaboration
Community Site Services
Compliance & Risk Management
Content Management
Customer Relationship Management
Dispatch Management
Document Management
eCommerce
eLearning
Electronics Design Automation (EDA)
Enterprise Resource Planning (ERP)
Expense Management
Help Desk Management

oin Our Mailing List [Go]

owplace Best Practices Portal
sted in Managed Services?
Managed Services Showplace®.
Kstrategies, Inc. • 2005-2009
Policies

FIGURE 5.2 A screenshot from the SaaS ShowPlace® showing the application categories menu (January 2010)

How to find PaaS providers

There are directories of Platform as a Service vendors on Cloudbook at http://www.cloudbook.net/products-platform where they list providers under the following subcategories:

- Horizontal Development (http://www.cloudbook.net/paas-horizontal);

- Vertical Development (http://www.cloudbook.net/paas-vertical);

- Media Platforms (http://www.cloudbook.net/paas-media);

- Cloud Services Management (http://www.cloudbook.net/paas-services-management);

- Middleware & Applications (http://www.cloudbook.net/paas-middleware-applications);

- Data Integration (http://www.cloudbook.net/paas-data-integration);

- Test Environments (http://www.cloudbook.net/paas-test).

How to find IaaS providers

The Cloudbook website also lists Infrastructure as a Service providers in its directory of cloud products and services under the category of 'Compute & Storage', which has the following subcategories.

- Infrastructure as a Service (http://www.cloudbook.net/iaas);

- Backup & Disaster Recovery (http://www.cloudbook.net/iaas-backup);

- Managed Hosting (http://www.cloudbook.net/iaas-hosting);

- Infrastructure Software (http://www.cloudbook.net/iaas-software);
- Physical Cloud Resources (http://www.cloudbook.net/iaas-resources);
- Security Resources (http://www.cloudbook.net/iaas-security);
- Operations Software & Services (http://www.cloudbook.net/iaas-operations).

Building your own cloud

Cloudbook.net is also a useful resource if your business is considering building its own cloud and, perhaps, even becoming a cloud computing provider. Firstly, as the name of the website suggests, there is a *free book* called *Cloud: Seven Clear Business Models* that is available to read online. Secondly, unless your business is an established enterprise, and maybe even then, you will need a data centre, network connectivity and perhaps some help from third parties. At http://www.cloudbook.net/directories/products-services-directory Cloudbook provides lists of 'cloud enablers', including consultants, system integrators and analysts; co-location service providers; and network service providers. You may not be able to find a local provider in this directory but you will gain an understanding of the kinds of services offered.

CLIENT REFERENCES

If the cloud computing providers you are considering provide a good service then they should have a number of case studies listed on their website. If you are in any doubt about their credentials and you are considering investing time and money in their services then why not contact some of the case study clients, preferably ones based in your own country, to hear their opinion first-hand? Search the internet for any reviews, too. You cannot stop customers from blogging or tweeting when they have something to complain about!

SERVICE LEVEL AGREEMENTS

In this section I discuss service level agreements (SLAs) drawing on my own experience of managing a cloud computing business and reworking its SLA, but also borrowing a number of ideas from a ZDNet.com article by Frank Ohlhorst (Ohlhorst, 2009).

By its nature a cloud computing purchase is usually impersonal and automated. You typically buy a service online and pay as you go, and there is often no way to negotiate a service level agreement – you just get the standard one that every customer gets unless your business is enterprise class and you are considering a serious investment. Moreover, most suppliers create SLAs to protect themselves, not their customers, against litigation, and, typically, they only offer customers minimal assurances. Understandably this state of affairs deters many would-be cloud customers, but some SLAs are better than others and there are a number of things to look out for in the small print. There are three key areas to consider when you are reviewing SLAs and talking to suppliers: data protection; continuity of service; and Quality of Service (QoS).

Data protection

If you store business data in public clouds then system security failures and data loss are obvious risks, and there may be legal risks, too (see Chapter 3). In any case this data is your responsibility and you would not want it to be stolen or lost, so there follow five sets of questions on data protection for you or your legal team to bear in mind when you are reading the Service Level Agreement of a cloud provider. The five sets of questions cover the issues of ownership; security; access; storage; and retrieval. If you are in a highly regulated industry or you handle sensitive data then you will need satisfactory answers to many if not all of these questions because you, not your provider, are legally responsible for protecting your data.

First, on *data ownership*:

- Is there agreement that *you* own your data and any software you develop on the provider's systems?
- Who owns the data about your data, such as access and modification log files?

Second, on *data security*:

- How many data centres does the provider have and how are they secured physically?
- How are data encrypted?
- How are their customers' data and backup files segregated?
- Is security continually tested as they develop and improve their systems?
- Can they produce evidence to show that their security systems have been externally audited and certified?

Third, on *data access*:

- What personnel policies do they have, and are background checks carried out on new employees?

- How is access controlled and logged?

- What access, if any, do system administrators have to your data?

- What access control reporting facilities do they provide for audit trails?

- Do they permit any subcontractors or partners to access their systems?

- Do they use two-factor authentication for remote access (see Chapter 3)?

Fourth, on *data storage*:

- How, and in what format, are data backed up, and where are the backups stored?

- Are data ever stored on third-party systems?

- Are data stored only in countries that subscribe to Safe Harbour agreements?

- What happens to data copies when an agreement is terminated?

- What happens to data copies if the provider's business fails?

- Do they offer the facility for periodic offline data backups, and, if so, what measures are in place to prevent unauthorized backups?

- Can specific data retention policies be applied for regulatory purposes?

- What is their disaster recovery plan?

And, fifth, on *data retrieval* for legal purposes:

- What procedures do they follow in the event of international or domestic government inquiries into data stored on their systems?

- Do they provide assurances that your data will not be compromised or seized if another of their customers is under legal investigation?

- Do their systems satisfy your internal requirements for governance and compliance?

- What facility for litigation searches or *electronic discovery* can they provide to investigators?

- How quickly can data preservation or production requests be satisfied?

- What costs will be charged by the provider to customers under investigation?

Continuity of service

Part of the appeal of cloud computing services is that you can access them at any time, but problems do occur (see the section on cloud outages in Chapter 3) and sometimes systems have to be taken temporarily offline for upgrades and maintenance (scheduled downtime), but you can typically expect a guaranteed uptime of between 99.5 per cent and 99.9 per cent from a provider. Now, SLAs are full of legalese, but they should contain details on systems outages, and if you want to gain a better understanding of how the provider deals with outages, here are some good questions to ask:

- What notice period do they have to give before any scheduled downtime?

- How often do they have scheduled downtime and how much time is usually involved?

- How are complete service outages and partial systems outages defined?

- How do customers report service problems – is there a ticketing system in place?

- How do they measure downtime and the severity of outages?

- How are customers compensated for outages?

- What redundancy is built into the systems to minimize outages?

- Do they have alternative methods for accessing data if an outage is prolonged?

- Do they provide reports on outages and other problems?

Quality of Service

Just as you would expect a Quality of Service (QoS) level for IP telephony or your broadband connection, you should also expect a desktop-like experience for Software as a Service and Platform as a Service, with no noticeable latency; and consistently fast provisioning of computing resources from Infrastructure as a Service. The supplier is not responsible for your internet connection or your local network, but they are responsible for the availability of their services and the performances of their cloud infrastructure. If your potential supplier's Service Level Agreement (SLA) does not cover QoS to your satisfaction then here are some questions to ask them about availability and performance:

- If additional resources are allocated dynamically to an overloaded application or server, how quickly does this happen?

- If a server instance fails, how quickly is it rebooted or replaced?

- Where in the world are the services hosted and how do the response times differ between geographical regions?

- Does the failure or poor performance of an individual application or server instance count as an outage for SLA purposes?

- Do they provide customers with monitoring tools for individual servers, applications and the cloud as a whole, and are these tools external?

- What general QoS metrics do they measure, if any?

As it is difficult to determine where the fault lies when using a service based on the internet, here are a few things you can do to understand and maximize QoS:

- Test and monitor your local internet connections (packet transmission speed, packet loss and response latency) during peak times, and measure data transfer speeds between your local networks and your chosen cloud – your Internet Service Provider may be able to help you improve connectivity.

- If you are migrating software from your private network to the cloud you can benchmark the performance of affected applications and operations on a powerful local server and network first, and then see what effect variations in memory and storage have on the performance by virtualizing the local server. What performance level and response time are acceptable for end users?

- Test your applications in the cloud, compare the performance with your local setup and document the differences. Can your cloud-based system deliver acceptable performance?

A very useful (and free!) tool for testing the performance of web-based applications and multi-page transactions is KITE, the Keynote Internet Testing Environment (http://kite.keynote.com/). You use the tool to navigate through a website and record the process as a 'script', and then you can re-run this script locally (from your PC) and from five geographically separate locations in the KITE network to compare its performance. If, however, you want to continually monitor your applications there is a charge for that Software as a Service product; and there are other products on the market, including CapCal (http://www.capcal.com/), a web scalability and performance testing application that runs on Amazon EC2 servers.

Quality of Service is a subjective term, but if you can define *objective* performance measurement tests and repeat them on a regular basis then you will be more likely to spot any gradual degradation of cloud services and bring them to the attention of your supplier. And if you can use your supplier's own measurement tools to prove your point then you will be in a stronger position. Whether you can negotiate an SLA on the basis of QoS will probably depend on the size and influence of your organization, but it could be worth a try, and it is certainly worth monitoring your systems because you are sharing a public cloud with an increasing number of tenants and you are relying on your supplier to ensure their cloud's capacity grows with demand.

SERVICE COSTS

With public cloud computing you pay only for the computing resources you use or subscribe to. This makes budgeting easier if you understand your supplier's price structure and you can predict confidently your usage. I will discuss the price structures of the three main service models below, but, before I do that, here are some more questions to ask your potential providers:

- What computing resources are chargeable?
- Is there a minimum price to pay per month?
- Are there additional costs for support?
- Are there any taxes or third-party services to pay for?
- Are the prices likely to change and what notice period is given?
- Are there any additional costs for software licences or operating systems?
- Are there any charges for retrieving and transferring data on terminating the agreement?
- Any other hidden costs?

Software as a Service costs

With Software as a Service (SaaS) you *usually pay* for the applications you use and the users you entitle to use them, and you pay per user per month, although in some cases you have to pay for at least a minimum number (five, for example) of users. Often the SaaS provider will offer a number of editions of their service at different prices, with varying functionality and levels of support – see Figure 5.3 for an example. You also pay for any additional data you store on the system in any given month that exceeds an initial data storage allowance. Now, I was careful to write 'usually pay' in the first sentence of this paragraph because you can gain limited access to some SaaS systems for free, which is great for small businesses who can get by very well with these systems until they hire more employees or accumulate a large amount of data – and then they can start paying. I have listed below three popular SaaS applications or application suites that were, at the time of writing, initially free of charge:

- Dropbox (http://www.dropbox.com) affords online file storage (first 2GB free), file access and file sharing, automatic synchronization with PCs and laptops, and offline access to tagged files on an iPhone.

- Google Apps (http://apps.google.com/) provides e-mail, office applications, file storage, document sharing and online chat tools, and is free for up to 50 users.

- Zoho (http://www.zoho.com) offers a huge range of SaaS applications from e-mail to web conferencing tools that are initially free for a small number of users.

Choose the edition that's right for your business

Our Most Popular Edition!

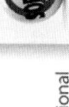 **Contact Manager**

Manage your business contacts and customers

£3/user/month

7 day free trial

 **Group**

Get started with basic CRM for small groups

£17/user/month

14 day free trial

 **Professional**

See a complete picture of your customer interactions

£45/user/month

30 day free trial

 **Enterprise**

Customize and integrate CRM for your unique needs

£85/user/month

30 day free trial

 **Unlimited**

Get unlimited power to run CRM and your entire business

£170/user/month

30 day free trial

Web-based Contact Manager
- Up to 5 users
- Store contacts
- Track customers
- Run activity reports
- Manage tasks and meetings
- Works with any email application, including Outlook & Gmail
- 99.9% availability

Includes everything in Contact Manager, PLUS:
- Up to 5 users
- Capture Web site leads
- Track sales opportunities
- Run sales reports
- Get real-time dashboards
- 12c5 phone support*
- Google AdWords tracking

Includes everything in Group, PLUS:
- No user limit
- Reports and analytics
- Custom dashboards
- Support case tracking
- Mass email
- Sales forecasting
- Mobile access
- Privacy controls
- Campaign management‡

Includes everything in Professional, PLUS:
- Workflow and approvals
- API for application integration
- Advanced security
- Content library‡
- Offline access
- Sales territory management
- Development sandbox for custom applications

Includes everything in Enterprise, PLUS:
- 24x7 Premier Support
- Dedicated administrator
- Full sandbox environment for testing and training
- Full mobile access
- Unlimited customization
- Unlimited development
- Increased storage limits †

* Excludes holidays
† Group Edition has 1GB total storage for data and files. Professional and Enterprise Editions have 20MB of data and 100MB of file storage/user. Unlimited Edition has 120MB of data and 100MB of file storage/user
‡ Special offer ends 300410

FIGURE 5.3 A screenshot for Salesforce.com editions and prices (March 2010)

Platform as a Service costs

Platform as a Service (PaaS) is a bit more complicated than Software as a Service, but it is often initially free for developers. For example, Google App Engine, at the time of writing, allows *applications* to use up to 6.5 CPU hours per day and transfer up to a gigabyte a day. Beyond these limits Google App Engine customers are charged for the following services on a monthly basis (see http://code.google.com/appengine/docs/billing.html for current prices):

- outgoing bandwidth per gigabyte (GB);
- incoming bandwidth per GB;
- compute time per CPU hour;
- stored data per GB;
- number of e-mails sent.

The Force.com PaaS has a different pricing structure from Google, ranging from one free, and very limited, user account to a monthly charge for a fully supported user (see Figure 5.4, and for current prices go to http://www.salesforce.com/), and on a monthly basis they charge for:

- number of users;
- number of applications;
- number of database objects;
- storage (GB);
- access to accounts and contacts databases in your Salesforce.com CRM;
- a level of technical support.

Get started with Force.com for free

 **Force.com Free**

Build and run your first cloud computing application

Free

Get started for free

Your first application for free:

- 1 free application
- 100 free users
- Up to 10 database objects
- 1 GB storage
- Developer sandbox
- Complete cloud platform
- Secure and reliable cloud infrastructure

Force.com Enterprise

Deliver multiple cloud applications to your enterprise

£34/user/month

Get started for free

Everything in Free, PLUS:

- Up to 10 applications
- Expand beyond 100 users
- Up to 200 database objects
- Access to CRM accounts & contacts
- Increased storage

Force.com Unlimited

Unlimited cloud computing for your entire business

£51/user/month

Get started for free

Everything in Enterprise, PLUS:

- Unlimited apps per user
- 24x7 premier support
- Dedicated administrator
- Full mobile access
- 2,000 database objects
- Increased storage

FIGURE 5.4 A screenshot of Force.com editions and prices (March 2010)

Infrastructure as a Service costs

Infrastructure as a Service (IaaS) price structures are far more complicated than SaaS or PaaS because of the range of choices and the amount of control over the infrastructure given to the customer. For example, in Amazon Web Services customers can be charged on a monthly usage basis for:

- number of compute hours for a particular server specification, which could be small, medium or large, say, with a choice of Linux, Windows or other operating systems;
- file storage per gigabyte and volume;
- number of IP addresses;
- GB of data transferred in and out of servers, storage, databases or message queues;
- number of input and output requests for data transfer;
- servers and processing power used in elastic load balancing;
- GB of data stored in particular data centre locations for quick downloads in geographical regions;
- number of server instances of a particular specification in a grid computing cluster and the number of hours used by that cluster;
- a level of technical support;
- import or export to physical storage devices per terabyte and device.

The Amazon Web Services (AWS) website provides an online calculator to help you estimate your monthly bill for each of the services they provide, along with examples of typical monthly prices for common use cases such as, for example, a High Performance Computing (HPC) cluster or a marketing website. See Figure 5.5 for a screenshot of the AWS calculator (http://calculator.s3.amazonaws.com/calc5.html) taken in January 2010. Other IaaS providers provide similar tools, including Microsoft who go a step further with their 'TCO and ROI Calculator' for Windows Azure (http://www.microsoft.com/windowsazure/tco/).

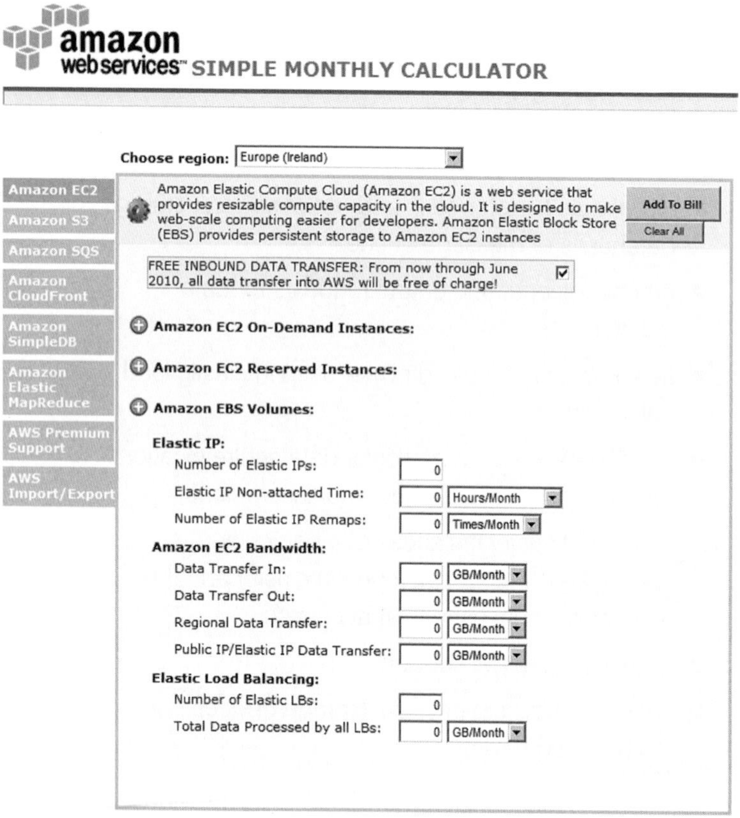

FIGURE 5.5 A screenshot from the AWS Simple Monthly Calculator (January 2010)

PROCESSES, PRACTICES AND STANDARDS

Although the potential for cloud computing is exciting and the suppliers are often innovative, agile and dynamic – constantly adding new features to their products – it is worth checking that they are doing the 'boring stuff', too. If your internal IT systems are subject to information governance policies then these policies need to be extended to your cloud-based systems, and you should expect your cloud provider to take the same care with their systems as your business does with its own. Here are some questions to ask your provider about their processes and practices:

- Do they follow any industry best practices for IT service management such as, for example, ITIL (IT Infrastructure Library)?

- Have their internal controls of IT systems and processes been independently audited to SAS 70 standards and can you have a copy of the audit report?

- Do they have ISO 27001 certification for their Information Security Management System?

But even if your data is in good hands you may want to switch cloud provider or move your cloud-based systems in-house at some point so you should ask your provider about *open cloud standards*, too – see the section on vendor lock-in in Chapter 3.

SUMMARY AND CHECKLIST

Finding cloud computing providers is not too difficult. There are a number of online directories; and after reading this book you should have a reasonable understanding of your technology choices. This chapter has described a number of things to look out for when selecting a cloud computing provider, and I have summarized the key points for supplier selection in the checklist below.

KEY SUMMARY POINTS AND CHECKLIST

Is the provider's Service Level Agreement negotiable?

Are the expected system availability and the measured Quality of Service acceptable?

Have you checked the provider's client references?

Can they provide satisfactory answers to your data protection questions?

Are the total monthly service costs affordable for your maximum expected usage?

Does the provider follow industry best practices for IT service management?

Are their systems and processes independently certified?

Can your systems and data be migrated easily to another provider's cloud?

QUESTION

If you can answer 'yes' to all or most of the questions in the checklist above then the supplier is worth considering; but there is one very important question left to answer: Is your business subject to regulatory compliance or internal governance restrictions that may prevent you from using cloud computing services? If your answer is 'yes' then I refer you back to the five sets of data protection questions listed earlier in this chapter and I recommend that you consult your legal department.

ACTIVITY

If you are already considering a particular cloud provider you could download and read through their standard SLA and see if you can find any points that need clarification or any issues raised in this chapter that they have not covered to your satisfaction.

CHAPTER 6
MOVING INTO THE CLOUD

There is nothing wrong with change, if it is in the right direction.

Winston Churchill, former British Prime Minister, 1874–1965

As we have seen in the preceding chapters, cloud computing has the potential to quickly address many business requirements for IT systems without significant capital expenditure. So should you pick a public cloud and move all your business processes into it without delay; move in gradually, taking advantage of cloud technologies without disrupting your business too much; replicate cloud technologies internally; or stick with what you have now? This chapter will suggest a five-step process for moving your business into the cloud, covering the following steps in turn:

1 Investigation

2 Evaluation

3 Decision

4 Implementation

5 Iteration.

STEP 1: INVESTIGATION

If your company is very small then a move to cloud computing may be an easy choice to make, but the larger your company gets the more difficult it becomes to make quick decisions about IT strategy and where your data is stored (see Chapter 4). As a first step, small businesses may consider performing a full business review while larger businesses will be more concerned with reviewing their information governance policies and processes; but understanding your current IT capabilities and costs is an essential starting point for businesses of all sizes; and before you search for a cloud computing solution you need to find a 'problem' to solve.

Business review

Even if you are simply looking to cut costs for one particular business function it may be helpful to look at your business as a whole because you may be able to do things better as well as more cheaply. Moreover, it may help you formulate a longer-term strategy for cloud computing adoption. Here are a few general tips to get you started:

- Review the key objectives and targets for your business, choosing SMARTA objectives, that is: Specific, Measurable, Achievable, Realistic, Timely and Agreed.

- Consider all parts of your business, including management; human resources; sales and marketing; operations; and finance.

- Ask your employees which tasks they spend most time on and what improvements could be made to give them more time for the tasks that are most important to your business.

- Ask your customers what you do well, where there is room for improvement, and what products you may be missing.

- Draw diagrams of your current work processes, document your current practices, and find out where the bottlenecks are.

- Look at your business objectives again and see if any improvements in working practices or processes could help you meet them.

If you do this well and engage your employees and customers then you may get a few more ideas for improving your business; or you may find that you have more serious problems to solve than reducing your IT costs! The engagement part of a business review is difficult because people are often suspicious when they are asked questions and when change is being discussed, but introducing change without consultation is also difficult. Finally, if you had not identified opportunities for your business at the start of your internal review you may have some ideas now, and after reading this book your ideas may involve cloud computing.

Information governance

Engagement is important in large organizations, too, and when cloud computing is being considered it is your IT department that most needs to be engaged. It is all too easy for non-technical staff in business units to bypass internal IT and begin using external cloud computing services, but that means bypassing established information governance policies and processes, too, and exposing your business to undue risk. This may save time and money in the short term but the long-term repercussions for your business could potentially be catastrophic. It is imperative that your internal information controls are extended to encompass external systems; but if your existing controls need improving then there are software tools to help you such as the Control & Risk Calculator (CRC), a free online tool for compliance, risk, and audit management (http://www.t2pa.com/crc).

IT systems review

Following your internal review you may have concrete objectives for your business that technology may help you to meet, but you should take stock of your current IT systems first. Starting with a particular business function or taking your business as a whole, you can document the following:

- hardware assets, with associated costs for power, rack space, maintenance contracts, and renewal;
- software assets, with licence costs, upgrade costs and user numbers;
- data storage, which may include offline storage on PCs;
- internet connectivity and usage;
- key technical people and their relevant skills;
- technical support requirements;
- user details, including their physical locations.

After documenting your IT setup and calculating the Total Cost of Ownership (TCO) you can then look to get answers to the following probing questions:

- Are there simple changes you can make to your current IT systems to improve failing processes and practices?
- Do your systems have sufficient redundancy and failover mechanisms?
- Can you work effectively from home or on the move if necessary?
- Do you have a tried and tested disaster recovery plan?
- Can your systems scale quickly if required?

If the answer to any of these questions is 'no' then cloud computing is worth considering, but IT systems depend on people, too. In order to prepare for cloud computing you may need to change the way that your employees think about IT. Encourage IT staff in particular to associate themselves with particular skills and functionality such as data processing, business intelligence or financial management, rather than particular software packages they have become used to. Communicate the benefits of cloud computing to all your staff and involve them in the decision-making process from the very beginning by asking them to find and test services for themselves, and rewarding them if they identify a low-risk solution that works well and saves money.

If you would like to see a detailed TCO analysis comparing NetSuite's CRM public cloud solution with an on-premise installation of Microsoft Dynamics CRM, I refer you to the white paper from Hurwitz Associates (Aggarwal and McCabe, 2009).

Problem selection

Once you understand your business objectives, along with the true cost and value of your IT systems to your business, then you may have a list of operations or processes that you could potentially perform (or problems to solve) using Infrastructure, Platform or Software as a Service. If we consider all these to be 'problems' then why not start by finding the problem upon which you believe a cloud computing solution could potentially have the *most impact* with the *least effort*? To help you make this decision here are some impact criteria to rate problems against, which I have grouped into two lists – one positive and one negative.

Positive impact criteria to score from 1 to 5:

- financial savings from cloud computing;
- customer pain caused by the problem;
- urgency of problem;
- team interest or buy-in;
- management interest or support.

Negative impact criteria to score from 1 to 5:

- resources required (money and people for example);
- effect on other systems (dependencies);
- difficulty of solving in a public cloud;
- time required to solve;
- data sensitivity.

For each business 'problem' take the sums of each list of criteria and divide the positive impact criteria sum by the negative impact criteria sum to give a ratio, and then multiply this ratio by 5 to give an *impact criteria rating* from 1 to 25. The problem that has the highest estimated impact criteria rating for your business is probably the best one to choose for your first cloud computing project.

STEP 2: EVALUATION

In Chapter 3 some of the main risks of cloud computing were described, and Chapter 5 provided tips on vendor selection, but before disregarding internal IT solutions you should ensure that you understand the true costs and benefits of cloud-based alternatives. And make sure you fully understand the problem you identified in Step 1 before you choose a solution.

Requirements gathering

Once you have selected a problem to solve you need to gather more detailed, measurable and testable requirements for a solution. You can start by consulting a limited number of relevant operational, technical and management staff, along with any other relevant stakeholders, including customers and suppliers, if appropriate. Discuss the details of the proposed project with these stakeholders and document their combined wish list for features, functionality and process improvements. What will the solution do in functional terms (create invoices, for example) and what will its key characteristics be in non-functional terms (regulatory compliance, for example)? Create a checklist of these functional and non-functional requirements in spreadsheet form and consider assigning a priority to each according to the MoSCoW method, where:

M = must have this;

S = should have this if at all possible;

C = could have this if it does not affect anything else;

W = won't have this time, but would like in the future.

As for characteristics, document for each requirement a clear description, the rationale behind it, the 'owner' and the beneficiaries. And make sure that all stakeholders sign off on the requirements documentation. Now, armed with a spreadsheet you are in a position to compare different solutions to your problem. Are there any cloud computing services that meet your needs?

Costing clouds

If your business is small with no formal information controls or compliance obligations then the internal costs of procuring cloud services are relatively low. But if you represent a large organization you may have information governance, risks and compliance to worry about so your solution evaluation costs will be higher due to the necessary involvement of your internal security and legal teams. There may also be training and documentation costs if a new IT system is to be implemented. So when you calculate the costs of cloud computing make sure you factor in your associated internal costs as well as your estimated service consumption costs.

Cloud testing

In the case of Infrastructure or Platform as a Service your IT team will be able to test the features, functionality and performance of these systems and report back. As for Software as a Service, ask some of your operational staff to test the applications, and try them yourself, too, while your IT team tests performance levels. If you have not ruled out a cloud computing solution at this stage then, hopefully, one service will stand out as the best for your business.

STEP 3: DECISION

Bearing in mind the points made in the previous chapters, you should select the provider and the service that best fit your current requirements and give you room to evolve. You are looking for a suitable, sustainable solution that gives you a financial Return on Investment and measurably high levels of performance. And remember that cloud computing is not just about *saving money*; it is about *making money*, too. Process improvements may lead to a requirement for fewer staff, while a new Customer Relationship Management system may coincide with a sales push and expansion.

Decisive factors

There may be reasons why cloud computing is not right for a particular application in your business. Drawing on previous chapters on risks, benefits, and service provider selection, here are a number of key factors to consider:

- Is there a genuine business case for adopting a cloud computing solution?

- Do you understand the Total Cost of Ownership and the expected Return on Investment?

- Do you have a need for IT systems that scale up and down with usage or user numbers?

- Is operational expenditure preferred to capital expenditure in this case?

- Is your application not business critical, and is occasional downtime acceptable?

- Does the solution satisfy your data protection and industry compliance requirements, if any?

- Does the solution fit well with your preferred technologies, development platforms or programming languages, if any?

- Can you easily integrate the solution with your favourite desktop software or other cloud solutions?

- Are the security risks in your chosen cloud acceptably low?

- Are the application performance levels consistently acceptable?

- Is mobile or remote access to affected data and applications acceptable and beneficial to your business?

- Does the new system enable business users to be more productive and less reliant on internal IT staff?

- Can you extract all your data from the system in a structured form that preserves its meaning whenever you need to?

If the answer to any of these questions is 'no' then the solution may not be appropriate. If, however, you have answered 'yes' to all those questions you consider important then the next step is implementation.

STEP 4: IMPLEMENTATION

Depending on the scale of your project and the size of your organization, the implementation of a cloud computing solution may take anything between an hour and a year, or even longer. Assuming the project is significantly large you will need a plan and a management strategy for it, and when the solution is fully implemented it will need measuring and monitoring.

Implementation plan

If you completed the evaluation step described above you will know what you hope to achieve with your project and who the stakeholders are, but it is advisable to write it all down. Any project that is not open-ended needs well-defined objectives, so the implementation plan for the project should include:

- Project definition – key business drivers, guiding principles and clear business objectives;

- Governance – named executive sponsors and project management team members;

- Project delivery team – named IT staff and business users who will implement, test, develop and use the system;

- Scope – deliverables specified in the requirements checklist and constrained by internal information governance;

- Implementation schedule – phases, activities, milestones and timescales;

- Work breakdown structure – details of scheduled activities and who will perform them;

- Resource requirements – budget plan for internal IT and staff costs and external cloud computing services;

- Risk management – ongoing assessment of risks;

- Stakeholder engagement – consultations and communications with business users;

- Quality assurance – key success metrics and service level monitoring (see Chapter 5).

Regarding project scope and resource requirements in the preceding list, if your business is small then you may decide to roll out the cloud computing service as soon as possible, but if you are responsible for a large organization then a *pilot project* may be more appropriate. In either case you may need answers to the following questions:

- Will this project be a pilot, and will it be rolled out to one site or multiple sites?
- How many users will be affected?
- If the project is a success are staffing levels likely to be affected?
- Does the product require any customization or integration?
- Is any additional infrastructure or connectivity required to support a cloud service?
- Are any mobile devices or thin client terminal devices required for testing purposes?
- What level of availability and performance is required of the service (see Chapter 5)?

And if a new system is to be introduced then the following points need to be included in the work breakdown part of the implementation plan:

- user training;
- data migration;
- customization;
- parallel running of old and new systems;
- integration with other systems;
- performance testing;
- user testing and documentation;
- security testing;
- ROLLBACK (exit) plan;

Project management

Use whatever project management methods you are comfortable with, but keep business objectives and the project's 'guiding principles' in mind. Depending on the project, whether it is Infrastructure, Platform or Software as a Service, you could either adhere rigidly to a functional specification and ensure there is no 'feature creep' or take a more *agile* approach to the project, involving key members of the project team at key stages and finding the best solution rather than the solution you originally envisaged. In any case you should communicate regularly with stakeholders; and it is always good practice to ask your technical staff to document what they do and let end users document the user experience as it develops. This will make training other users much easier.

Monitoring and measuring

If you are using Infrastructure as a Service (IaaS) then you can monitor the performance of your systems in great detail at a low level. As for Platform as a Service and Software as a Service, or applications running on IaaS, the user experience can be monitored by timing and recording common web transactions on a regular basis, using automated tools or manually (see Chapter 5). Besides performance, it is important to monitor user adoption of any new systems you introduce. It is no good having a new Customer Relationship Management system, for example, if your sales team are not using it; but if you involve users at the development stage of a new system then they are more likely to adopt it.

Exit plan

Not all projects are completed successfully and some systems turn out to be less useful than you expect, so if your use of a particular cloud technology is to be long term (Enterprise Resource Planning, for example) rather than temporary (data crunching, for example), it is in your interest to ensure your business has a way back and a way out. Often businesses choose to use a new system in parallel with the old one for a fixed period of time so that data in the old system is kept up-to-date, just in case the business needs to revert to the old system, but you may be able to keep the two systems synchronized automatically without double entry. That is a way back, but what about a way out? Well, if you read the checklist at the end of Step 3 you will see that the final question is 'Can you extract all your data from the system in a structured form that preserves its meaning whenever you need to?' With web services this should be possible, but be sure to put your system to the test because it is *your data* after all.

STEP 5: ITERATION

Assuming your first project was a success then you may decide to move more of your business activities into public clouds. Armed with your experience of the previous four steps you can repeat the process, continually iterate and improve. Are your business goals still the same? Have your systems improved? Has your new technology spawned any new ideas or new opportunities? What problems still remain to be solved? Which processes or operations still slow down your business? Do you have an evolving technology strategy that involves cloud computing?

SUMMARY

In many ways the process of moving into a public cloud is very similar to choosing and adopting any IT system; but because cloud systems are relatively easy to deploy it is tempting to take less care and less thought. This chapter has raised a number of points that may give you pause for thought.

KEY SUMMARY POINTS

 In the investigation and evaluation steps your aim is to understand where you are now with your current IT systems, where you want to go with your business, and whether cloud-based solutions are appropriate.

 Focus on specific objectives and resist changing too much at once.

 The decision and implementation steps are equally important because you want to make sure that the chosen solution performs acceptably well, and if it does not, or your requirements change, you should ensure that you have an exit plan in place.

Cloud computing enables your business to be agile and progressive so do not rest on your laurels after a successful project; iteration involves re-evaluation and more implementation projects to drive your business forward.

QUESTION

After reading this chapter, are you now ready to begin moving your business into the cloud or are you still unsure?

ACTIVITY

Begin with Step 1 and find a problem to solve in your business.

CHAPTER 7
CONCLUSION

We are in a big transition from a device-centric world to an information-centric world. It's going to be about how do you make the information useful and available and make that the centre of people's lives instead of specific devices. Devices will have to cleave to the information rather than the other way around. IT infrastructure, the plumbing, will fade away for most users and businesses, and will increasingly be left to professional providers.

Paul Maritz, VMware CEO, November 2008

This *Quick Start Guide* has discussed the meanings, the technologies, the benefits and the risks of cloud computing, and presented a number of common adoption scenarios. The case studies recounted success stories from a wide range of industry sectors and from companies of all sizes, while tips, tools and checklists were included to help you choose a provider and move your business into the cloud. But is cloud computing just a 'storm in a teacup' and will it soon be replaced by the next 'next big thing'? I honestly do not think so and I am not alone in my belief.

According to Microsoft research chief Rick Rashid, in 2009 around 20 per cent of all the servers sold around the world were being bought by a small handful of internet companies – namely, Microsoft, Google, Yahoo and Amazon (Waters, 2009). It is clear then that public clouds account for much of the computing that we already do and I expect us to do much more in public clouds – as businesses and as individuals. But private clouds, hybrid clouds and community clouds will also be prevalent. For example, the governments of both the United States of America (http://www.apps.gov/) and the United Kingdom (Arthur, 2010) have launched major *government cloud* initiatives. All this suggests to me that cloud computing is here to stay.

In this concluding chapter I will address the main obstacles to cloud computing adoption, predict how these and other problems will be overcome, and wrap up the book with ten top tips.

OBSTACLES TO ADOPTION

The financial incentives are clear (for small to medium-sized businesses anyway) so what are the main obstacles to cloud computing adoption? Chapter 3 described a number of key risks associated with cloud computing and suggested ways of mitigating these risks. Most of these risks surround data protection and security issues, which often prevent companies from purchasing cloud services. A 2009 survey by Hosting.com of company executives and IT professionals revealed very similar cloud computing adoption rates for smaller and larger companies, but security was more of a concern for larger companies (Hosting.com, 2009). But, aside from security, in my experience the two most common objections to cloud computing are internal resistance and internet dependency.

Internal resistance

Key people in IT departments may perceive cloud computing as a threat. They may fear losing control of key systems and they may even fear for their jobs. Their fears are well founded because one of the key benefits of cloud computing is that it can reduce the number of administration tasks that need to be carried out on back-end IT systems, but, on the other hand, it also frees up your IT staff to work more on front-end applications where there is potentially more business value to be gleaned. Chapter 6 provided a number of suggestions to help you engage with your staff while investigating cloud computing solutions.

Internet dependency

Perhaps the main issue with cloud computing is still the inherent dependency on the internet, but modern business persons are rarely far away from an internet connection. At home they have broadband, they connect their laptops using 3G or a public wireless network when they are on the road, and they have mobile devices running web browsers, e-mail clients and numerous business software applications. Moreover, despite the security risks within public clouds, your business is probably more likely to lose a laptop containing company data than to have data stolen from the cloud. If, however, you do choose a public cloud product with offline capabilities then it would be wise to employ data encryption tools or at least password protection on your local device.

PREDICTIONS

I believe the remaining objections to cloud computing will be overcome, and, again, I am not alone in my belief. In an article for ZDNet, Jason Hiner listed his 'Four reasons why business will take to the cloud' (Hiner, 2009). I am in agreement with Hiner, and I also have four more predictions of my own to add, so I have listed below *eight reasons* why I think cloud computing will eventually become the standard way for businesses to procure IT services:

1 Separation of data from applications will mean that applications can run in public clouds while the data can be stored (optionally) in private data centres.

2 Offline access for online applications – where data and applications can be cached on a local device and synchronized with online systems when connectivity is restored – will remove our complete dependency on the internet.

3 Ubiquitous mobile internet access and high-speed wireless connections will bring broadband connectivity to cars, buses and trains; and our mobile devices will continue to get smarter, too.

4 The financial benefits of moving capital expenditure to operational expenditure with pay-per-use services will still be the key reason for using cloud computing.

5 More service providers will adopt open standards for cloud interoperability.

6 Service providers will be expected to comply with information security standards and data protection legislation.

7 The environmental benefits that come with sharing resources and reducing business travel will make cloud computing the socially acceptable green alternative.

8 The success of small, agile, progressive businesses that iterate their IT systems and processes – using public clouds to quickly develop new and innovative

ways of doing things – will make other businesses take notice.

Only time will tell but I predict a sunny future for cloud computing.

TOP TEN TIPS

This book has been full of lists so we may as well end with one more! Here are my top ten tips for cloud computing adoption:

 1 Review your business and find appropriate 'problems' to solve using cloud computing.

 2 Engage with stakeholders throughout the business, including legal, finance and IT security.

 3 Review your IT systems, including your local network bandwidth, to ensure your business can operate in the cloud.

 4 Understand your data protection responsibilities and aim to minimize information risk.

 5 Forecast usage scenarios and total costs, including associated internal costs.

 6 Make a business case and get it signed off by relevant stakeholders.

7 Start with a small project but think big, keeping future systems integration and your IT strategy in mind.

 8 Find a provider that can support your requirements for information governance and service management.

 9 Monitor performance and service levels.

 10 Create an exit plan and make sure it works!

GLOSSARY

Any sufficiently advanced technology is indistinguishable from magic.

Arthur C Clarke, Profiles of The Future, *1961*

In the glossary below cross-references between glossary items are formatted in *italics*.

Ajax (Asynchronous JavaScript and XML) A group of interrelated web development techniques used to create feature-rich and interactive software applications in a web browser (such as *SaaS* applications) where data can be retrieved from a web server asynchronously using the *XMLHttpRequest* object and displayed dynamically using JavaScript in response to user interaction, without reloading a whole web page.

API (Application Programming Interface) An interface implemented within a software program (application) that enables programmers to access a specific set of its services from their own, external software programs.

cloud The internet as depicted in computer network diagrams to abstract the underlying infrastructure.

cloud broker A company that acts as an intermediary between their customers and multiple *cloud providers* to provide one or more of the following services: selecting the best provider or providers for particular requirements; negotiating prices; additional security; and service monitoring.

cloud bursting The manual or automatic expansion of a particular computing resource pool from a cloud of one deployment model (a *private cloud*, for example) into another (a *public cloud*, for example),

cloud commuter An employee who works remotely using *cloud computing* rather than travelling to an office.

cloud computing A model for enabling convenient, *on-demand* network access to a shared pool of configurable computing resources that can be rapidly provisioned and released with minimal management effort or service provider interaction.

cloud portability The facility to move applications and data from one *cloud provider* to another (see *vendor lock-in*).

cloud proliferation The situation and associated risks present when a customer is taking services from multiple *public clouds* (see *single sign-on*).

cloud provider A third-party service provider that supplies *cloud computing* services to multiple customers using the same *multi-tenanted* infrastructure.

cloud services See *service models*.

cloudsourcing Sourcing a complete set of cloud services for your business from one or more *cloud providers*.

cloud storage The services that enable entities to store their data in *public clouds* (a subcategory of *IaaS*).

cloudstorming The act of connecting multiple *public clouds*.

cloud washing The efforts of IT vendors to market their more traditional IT services as *cloud* services.

cluster A group of connected computer servers working together in parallel to perform a particular function as if they were a single larger computer.

community cloud A *cloud computing* environment shared by a particular community of organizations with common interests or data protection concerns.

compute grid A set of hardware and software that forms a compute infrastructure where compute-intensive batch applications are run (see also *data grid*).

consumption-based pricing A pricing model whereby a *cloud provider* charges its customers for the computing resources they consume, such as data storage or bandwidth, rather than a fixed monthly fee (see also *subscription-based pricing*).

Content Delivery Network (CDN) A system of networked computers containing copies of data placed at various geographical locations so as to maximize download speeds for clients in different parts of the world.

Content Distribution Network See *Content Delivery Network*.

CPU The Central Processing Unit (there can be more than one in a modern, multi-core computer processor) of a computer, which contains the electronics that carry out the instructions of a computer program within a maximum processing speed given in cycles per second or Hz.

CPU hour A measure of *cloud services* consumption that is equivalent to one hour's worth of instructions performed on a computer's *CPU*.

CRM Customer Relationship Management systems are used by companies to manage their sales processes, and there are many *SaaS* products available for CRM.

data grid The *IaaS* resources that provide seamless access to the local or remote data required to complete compute-intensive calculations (see also *compute grid*).

deployment models The four models, according to the *NIST*, are *public cloud*, *community cloud*, *private cloud* and *hybrid cloud*.

EC2 The Elastic Compute Cloud provided by Amazon Web Services is an example of *IaaS* where *elastic computing* and *on-demand computing* are provided through *self-service* provisioning of virtual *machine images*.

elastic computing The availability of computing resources that can expand and contract on demand – a key feature of *cloud computing*.

enterprise-class IT The capabilities afforded by high-end hardware and software systems, which were out of reach of small to medium-sized businesses until the emergence of *cloud computing*.

essential characteristics (of cloud computing) On-demand self-service, broad network access, resource pooling, rapid elasticity and measured service (according to the *NIST*).

external cloud A *public cloud* or *community cloud* provided by a *cloud provider*.

failover The capability to switch an online service automatically to a redundant or standby computer server, system, or network upon failure or abnormal termination of the service.

federated identity (see *single sign-on*).

follow-the-moon cloud A *global public cloud* that is configured to move customers' active application servers during their daytime working hours to time zones on the other side of the world where it is night-time and energy and data centre cooling are cheaper – the downside of follow-the-moon is that network latency is higher for customers than if the application servers were located nearer to them (see *follow-the-sun cloud*).

follow-the-sun cloud A *global public cloud* that is configured to move customers' application servers across time zones so that they have the lowest possible network latency during their standard working hours while the cloud as a whole makes optimum use of available infrastructure during a 24-hour period (see also *follow-the-moon cloud*).

Force.com The *PaaS* offering from Salesforce.com.

global public cloud A *public cloud* with data centres in multiple geographical locations around the world.

Google App Engine The *PaaS* offering from Google.

Google Apps The *SaaS* offering from Google that includes applications for business productivity and collaboration.

grid computing A computing architecture where computations can be split and data can be processed in parallel across a distributed network of computers (see *compute grid* and *data grid*).

home worker See *cloud commuter*.

horizontal development Software development within a *PaaS* environment that does not build on the data models of a core SaaS system (unlike *vertical development*).

hosted desktop An interactive, live screenshot of a fully functional computer desktop (usually Microsoft Windows) that is hosted in a *public cloud* and is accessible over the internet using a locally installed *thin client*; the desktop provides the user with access to company data and software applications from anywhere (as well as local file systems, shared network drives and printers) and it responds to key strokes and mouse movements as if it was installed on the user's hardware.

HTTP These four letters, which stand for HyperText Transfer Protocol, are found at the start of every unsecured website address and is the method by which all the standard elements that make up a web page (words and images, etc) are requested from a web server.

HTTPS Secure *HTTP* for encrypted web page requests such as in internet banking.

hybrid cloud A linked combination of a *private cloud* and a *public cloud*.

hypervisor The management software that allows multiple *virtual machines* (and their operating systems) to share the same hardware.

IaaS See *Infrastructure as a Service*.

information governance A set of policies, procedures, processes and controls for information management implemented by an organization to support their regulatory, legal, risk, environmental and operational requirements.

Infrastructure as a Service (IaaS) The *service model* that includes *virtual machines*, *cloud storage*, processing power, bandwidth and networking resources.

internal cloud See *private cloud*.

IP telephony Telephony services where voice messages are transmitted over the internet.

ITIL The Information Technology Infrastructure Library, which recommends best practices for the management and provision of IT services.

Java One of the widely used programming languages supported by *Google App Engine* and other *PaaS* systems.

machine image See *virtual appliance*.

mashup A web page or web application that combines data and/or functionality from multiple sources to create a new service.

middleware Software that connects two or more disparate software applications or software components.

multi-tenanted system A system (a *public cloud*, for example) shared with other consumers (tenants).

network latency Delays in application response time caused by the finite time it takes for data to travel over a network, which depends on the distance travelled and the number of hops – that is, intermediate devices – in between.

NIST The National Institute of Standards and Technology.

on-demand computing A service by which computing resources are made available to consumers upon request (a key feature of *cloud computing*).

one-time password A seemingly random password that is provided to a user by an external device as part of the log-on procedure for accessing an online service – the device contains a sequence of passwords that matches a sequence stored in a database for that user account and the online service (see *two-factor authentication*).

PaaS See *Platform as a Service*.

Patriot Act A statute passed into law by the United States government in 2001 that enables law enforcement agencies in the United States to search telephone, e-mail communications, medical, financial and other records for suspected links to terrorism – without a court order.

pay-per-use (or pay-as-you-go) The payment model used in cloud computing where consumers pay only for the computing resources they use (see *consumption-based pricing* and *subscription-based pricing*) and avoid capital investment in software and hardware.

Platform as a Service (PaaS) The *service model* that enables software developers to quickly create and develop scalable, database-driven web applications within an internet-based environment (*cloud*) where the web servers are configured and managed by the *cloud provider*.

private cloud The *deployment model* used internally by organizations.

public cloud The *deployment model* where services are provided by a *cloud provider*.

Public Key Infrastructure (PKI) The hardware and software required to manage the association of public key certificates (digital certificates) with user identities (private keys) for security purposes such as *two-factor authentication*.

Python One of the widely-used programming languages supported by *Google App Engine* and other *PaaS* systems.

REST (Representational State Transfer) A software architecture that is the basis of the worldwide web, and uses *HTTP* as a lightweight communication channel to enable resources such as web pages to be downloaded from a web server.

S3 (Simple Storage Services) *Cloud storage* provided by Amazon Web Services.

SaaS See *Software as a Service*.

Safe Harbour agreement A set of principles for data protection that numerous countries have officially approved.

self-service The capability for consumers to procure, deploy and access *cloud services* through a web browser or *web services* without communicating with the *cloud provider*.

service migration The act of moving from one *public cloud* to another (see *cloud portability*).

service models (of cloud computing) *SaaS*, *PaaS* and *IaaS*.

service provider See *cloud provider*.

single sign-on The ability to log on to multiple *cloud services* at the same time using a single user name and password at one entry point (also called *federated identity*).

SLA (Service level agreement) The part of a contractual agreement with a *service provider* that defines the level of service they will provide, including guarantees of availability and performance.

smart card A plastic card the size of a credit card that is provided to users of an online service and upon which is a unique security grid that has characters in specific coordinates that the user can be quizzed on when logging on to the service (see *two-factor authentication*).

SOAP (Simple Object Access Protocol) Used in *web services* to facilitate the exchange of *XML*-based messages over a network.

Software as a Service (SaaS) The *service model* by which feature-rich software applications (using techniques such as *Ajax*) are provided.

subscription-based pricing The pricing model whereby customers pay a fee to a *cloud provider* to use their service for a particular time period (see also *consumption-based pricing*).

thin client Lightweight, locally installed software used as a gateway to *cloud services* on remote servers (a web browser is the most common example).

thin client terminal A low-specification, energy-efficient computing device with a minimal operating system running *thin client* software to access *cloud services*.

two-factor authentication The use of a hardware or software method alongside usual login credentials (user name and password) for uniquely identifying a user when they log on to a computer system.

utility computing The idea that computing resources (and *cloud services*) can be provided 'on tap' like gas, water, telephony or electricity.

vendor lock-in The situation that arises when customer data and applications stored in one *public cloud* cannot be easily moved to another provider's cloud (see *cloud portability*).

vertical cloud A *cloud service* that is optimized for use in a particular vertical market such as education or financial services.

vertical development Software development within a *PaaS* environment that builds on the data models of a core *SaaS* system on the same platform (unlike *horizontal development*).

viral media Media such as online games and videos that become popular through the process of internet sharing.

virtual appliance A *virtual machine* with a particular set of software pre-installed.

virtualization The software methods (including *hypervisors*) used to allow multiple virtual computing resources to run on a single hardware platform (multiple *virtual machines* on a single hardware server, for example).

virtual machine A software *virtualization* of computer hardware that executes programs like a physical computer and can be interacted with like a physical computer.

virtual private cloud A private cloud computing environment running within a *public cloud* infrastructure.

virtual server A *virtual machine* used as a server.

web services The standard communication protocols, which include *SOAP* and *REST*, that are used to pass data to and from *cloud services* and to create *mashups*.

Windows Azure Microsoft's *PaaS* offering.

XML (eXtensible Markup Language) The text-based format used to define structured data as used in *web services*.

XMLHttpRequest An *API* available in web browser scripting languages such as JavaScript that is used to send *HTTP* or *HTTPS* requests directly to a web server and load the server response data directly back into the script in *XML* form so it can be used to dynamically change the current web page (of a *SaaS* application, for example) without reloading it.

REFERENCES

Aggarwal, S and McCabe, L (2009) [accessed 14 January 2010] 'The Compelling TCO Case for Cloud Computing in SMB and Mid-Market Enterprises: A total cost of ownership comparison of cloud and on-premise business applications', *Netsuite.com*, http://www.netsuite.com/portal/resource/collateral.shtml

Armbrust, M *et al* (2009) [accessed 10 November 2009] 'Above the Clouds: A Berkeley View of Cloud Computing', *University of California at Berkeley*, Technical Report No. UCB/EECS-2009-28, http://www.eecs.berkeley.edu/Pubs/TechRpts/2009/EECS-2009-28.html

Arthur, C (2010) [accessed 27 January 2010] 'Government to set up own cloud computing system', the *Guardian*, http://www.guardian.co.uk/technology/2010/jan/27/cloud-computing-government-uk

Austin, S (2009) [accessed 2 March 2010] 'Turning Out The Lights: Coghead', the *Wall Street Journal Blogs*, http://blogs.wsj.com/venturecapital/2009/02/19/turning-out-the-lights-coghead/

Boggs, R *et al* (2009) [accessed 10 March 2010] 'Reducing Downtime and Business Loss: Addressing Business Risk with Effective Technology', *IDC*, http://www.hp.com/hpinfo/newsroom/press_kits/2009/CompetitiveEdge/ReducingDowntime.pdf

Doctorow, C (2009) [accessed 10 January 2010] 'Not every cloud has a silver lining', the *Guardian*, http://www.guardian.co.uk/technology/2009/sep/02/cory-doctorow-cloud-computing

Donoghue, A (2009) [accessed 5 January 2010] 'EC Calls On Europe To Board Cloud Computing Train', *eWeek Europe*, http://www.eweekeurope.co.uk/news/ec-calls-on-europe-to-board-cloud-computing-train-2428

Farber, D (2008) [accessed 13 December 2009] 'Oracle's Ellison nails cloud computing', *CNET News*, http://news.cnet.com/8301-13953_3-10052188-80.html

Fried, I (2009) [accessed 8 January 2010] 'Sidekick outage casts cloud over Microsoft', *CNET.com*, http://news.cnet.com/8301-13860_3-10372525-56.html

Gottfrid, D (2007) [accessed 18 January 2010] 'Self-service, Prorated Super Computing Fun!', *New York Times Open Blogs*, http://open.blogs.nytimes.com/2007/11/01/self-service-prorated-super-computing-fun/

Greenpeace (2010) 'Make IT Green: Cloud Computing and its Contribution to Climate Change', *Greenpeace International*, http://www.greenpeace.org/raw/content/international/press/reports/make-it-green-cloud-computing.pdf

Hiner, J (2009) [accessed 24 January 2010] 'Four reasons why business will take to the cloud', *ZDNet.com*, http://resources.zdnet.co.uk/articles/comment/0,1000002985,39651447,00.htm

Hoff, T (2008) [accessed 18 January 2010] 'Scaling Bumper Sticker: A 1 Billion Page Per Month Facebook RoR App', *High Scalability*, http://www.highscalability.com/scaling-bumper-sticker-1-billion-page-month-facebook-ror-ap

Hosting.com (2009) [accessed 20 February 2010] '2009 Cloud Computing Trends Report', *Hosting.com*, http://hosting.com/cloudhosting/ebook/

Huddle (2008) [accessed 19 January 2010] 'Boots Huddles up for efficient working practices', *Huddle.com*, http://www.huddle.net/press/case-studies/

ITRC (2009) [accessed 14 February 2010] '2008 Data Breach Totals Soar', *IdentityTheft Resource Center*, http://www.idtheftcenter.org/artman2/publish/m_press/2008_Data_Breach_Totals_Soar.shtml

Joyent (2008) [accessed 18 January 2010] 'Scaling Rails to 1 Billion Page Views', Video case study, http://www.youtube.com/watch?v=p4Qtt0aU1L4

Kobie, N (2009) [accessed 18 January 2010] 'Guardian goes for Google Apps', *IT Pro*, http://www.itpro.co.uk/609839/guardian-goes-for-google-apps

Laird, P (2009) [accessed 11 January 2010] 'Cloud Computing Taxonomy at Interop Las Vegas, May 2009', *Laird OnDemand*, http://peterlaird.blogspot.com/2009/05/cloud-computing-taxonomy-at-interop-las.html

Mazzon, J (2009) [accessed 8 January 2010] 'On yesterday's email', *Official Google Docs Blog*, http://googledocs.blogspot.com/2009/03/on-yesterdays-email.html

McMullan, S (2008) [accessed 31 January 2010] 'Salesforce for Google Apps', *Google Blog*, http://googleblog.blogspot.com/2008/04/posted-by-scott-mcmullan-google-apps.html

Mell, P and Grance, T (2009) [accessed 12 December 2009] 'The NIST Definition of Cloud Computing', Version 15, 10-7-09, *National Institute of Standards and Technology Information Technology Laboratory*, http://csrc.nist.gov/groups/SNS/cloud-computing/cloud-def-v15.doc

Miller, R (2007) [accessed 21 February 2010] 'Amazon EC2 Outage Wipes Out Data', *Data Center Knowledge*, http://www.datacenterknowledge.com/archives/2007/10/02/amazon-ec2-outage-wipes-out-data/

Ohlhorst, F (2009) [accessed 15 December 2009] *ZDNet.co.uk*, http://reviews.zdnet.co.uk/software/enterpriseapplications/0,1000001813,39681045-2,00.htm

Pettey, C and Stevens, H (2009a) [accessed 18 January 2010] 'Gartner's 2009 Hype Cycle Special Report Evaluates Maturity of 1,650 Technologies', *Gartner.com*, http://www.gartner.com/it/page.jsp?id=1124212

Pettey, C and Stevens, H (2009b) [accessed 18 January 2010] 'Gartner Says Worldwide Cloud Services Revenue Will Grow 21.3 Percent in 2009', *Gartner.com*, http://www.gartner.com/it/page.jsp?id=920712

Robinson, J (2009) [accessed 18 January 2010] '*The Guardian* moves office into the cloud', *Information Age magazine*, March 2009 edition, http://www.information-age.com/channels/it-services/it-case-studies/1010747/the-guardian-moves-office-into-the-cloud.thtml

Ruiz, Y and Walling, A (2005) 'Home-based working using communication technologies', http://www.statistics.gov.uk/downloads/theme_labour/LMT_Oct05.pdf, Labour Market

Trends Volume 113, *Office for National Statistics*, October 2005

Salesforce.com (2004) [accessed 18 January 2010] 'Salesforce Deployment Results in Significant ROI at SunTrust; Capital Market Fees Up 67%', *Salesforce.com*, http://www.salesforce.com/uk/customers/financial-services/suntrust.jsp

Salesforce.com (2007) [accessed 20 January 2010] 'With an Integrated Salesforce CRM Solution, Google Improves Sales Tracking', *Salesforce.com*, http://www.salesforce.com/customers/communications-media/google.jsp

Salesforce.com (2008) [accessed 19 January 2010] 'By Building 2go on Force.com, CODA Delivers an Accounting Revolution', *Salesforce.com*, http://www.salesforce.com/platform/innovators/coda.jsp

Sclater, N (2010) [accessed 22 January 2010] 'OU adopts Google Apps for Education', *Sclater.com*, http://sclater.com/blog/?p=399

Sheehan, M (2008) [accessed 7 December 2009] 'Cloud Computing Expo: Introducing the Cloud Pyramid', *Cloud Computing Journal*, http://cloudcomputing.sys-con.com/node/609938

Twitter (2009) [accessed 12 February 2010] 'Monday Morning Madness', *Twitter Blog*, http://blog.twitter.com/2009/01/monday-morning-madness.html

VMWare (2010) [accessed 20 January 2010] 'Increase Energy Efficiency with Virtualization', *Vmware*, http://www.vmware.com/virtualization/green-it/

Waters, R (2009) [accessed 4 January 2010] 'How many computers does the world need?', *FT.com Tech Blog*, http://blogs.ft.com/techblog/2009/03/how-many-computers-does-the-world-need/

Williams, M (2008) [accessed 4 January 2010] 'Cloud Computing calls in the Credit Crunch', *Muon Cloud blog*, http://blog.muoncloud.com/2008/12/08/cloud-computing-calls-in-the-credit-crunch/

Williams, M (2009) [accessed 4 January 2010] 'Cloud computing commuters and the future of London', *Muon Cloud blog*, http://blog.muoncloud.com/2009/02/19/cloud-computing-commuters-future-of-london/

Williams, M (2010) [accessed 31 January 2010] 'Reported cloud outages for Amazon, Google, Microsoft and Salesforce.com in 2008 and 2009', *Muon Cloud blog*, http://blog.muoncloud.com/2010/01/31/reported-cloud-outages-for-amazon-google-microsoft-and-salesforce-com-in-2008-and-2009/

Zetter, K (2009) [accessed 12 February 2010] 'Weak Password Brings Happiness to Twitter Hacker', *Wired.com*, http://www.wired.com/threatlevel/2009/01/professed-twitt/

Zoho (2007) [accessed 18 January 2010] 'Oxfam America case study', *Zoho.com*, http://www.zoho.com/creator/casestudy/oxfam.pdf